BRAZIL

First published in 2013 by Goodman Fiell

This edition published in 2014 by SevenOaks

An imprint of the Carlton Publishing Group

20 Mortimer Street

London W1T 3JW

www.goodmanbooks.co.uk

A CIP catalogue record for this book is available from the British Library.

ISBN 978 1 78177 141 9

Printed in China

Carlton Books would like to offer their immense gratitude to Maria Luisa Cavalcanti for

her accomplished work on the image selection and captioning of this book.

Overleaf:

Aerial view of the Rio Negro and the Rio Solimões joining to form the Amazon river.

REGIS ST. LOUIS

BRAZIL

SevenOaks

CONTENTS

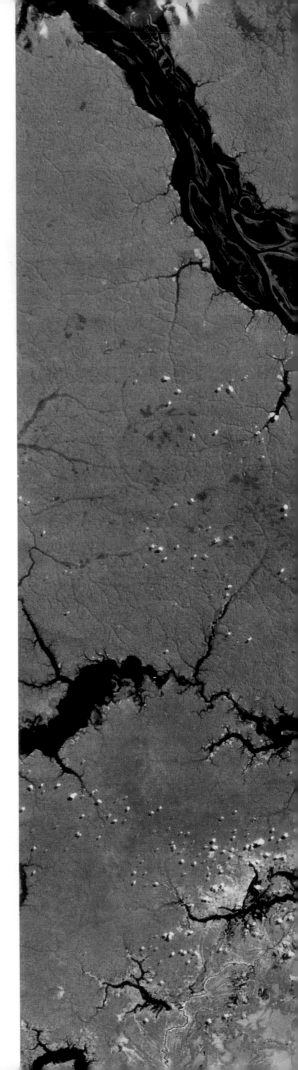

RIGHT A beach in the Japaratinga municipality of the state of Alagoas on the northeastern coast. Known for its outstanding natural beauty, the area is a major tourist destination.

INTRODUCTION

At last, the old jibe about Brazil being "the country of the future – and it always will be" can be laid to rest. With a burgeoning middle-class and a booming economy, the promising future so long delayed for Latin America's giant has finally arrived. By early 2013, Brazil had become the world's seventh largest economy, according to the International Monetary Fund (IMF). Its has also proved to be one of the fastest growing economies across the globe, expanding at an average annual rate of nearly 4 per cent since 2004, according to a report by the World Bank – this despite the massive global financial crisis that stymied almost all the world's major economies (during the same period the UK and the US in comparison grew by 1 per cent and 1.6 per cent respectively). Growth even climbed to 7.5 per cent in 2010, Brazil's highest level in 25 years. Unemployment has reached an historic low and the once vast disparity between rich and poor declined for each of the last 14 years, according to the CIA World Factbook.

What's even more surprising is how far Brazil has come in such a short time. Just a generation ago, a military dictatorship was running the show, censorship was rife and the inescapable curse of inflation spiralled ever higher, year after year. In the grip of high crime rates, stagnant growth, widespread corruption and a host of other problems, Brazil never seemed able to live up to its promise – a potential described by Stefan Zweig, an Austrian exile from the Nazis who settled in Brazil in 1940, where he wrote a bestseller about his newly adopted country entitled *Brazil: Country of the Future* (1941).

Most Brazilians credit the nation's dramatic turnaround to Luiz Inácio Lula da Silva (widely known as "Lula") – president from 2003 until the end of 2011. His approval ratings of 83 per cent when he left office are unmatched by any president in the Americas since the Second World War – and all the more surprising given his unlikely background. Born to a poor family in the sun-baked poverty-stricken state of Pernambuco in the Northeast, at a young age Lula migrated over 2,000 km (1,243 miles) to the bustling city of São Paulo, where he worked as a shoe-shiner, street vendor and lathe operator, having dropped out of school by the fifth grade to help support his family. In his twenties, he found work in an automobile factory, where he lost a finger in an accident. He got involved in labour activities in the 1970s, became a union leader, and in 1980 helped found the *Partido dos Trabalhadores* (PT, The Workers' Party): a mix of workers, left-wing academics and environmentalists. He was a vocal critic of the military regime — his involvement organizing strikes landed him in prison for a month in 1980. The manifesto of this progressive organization expressed the need "to build an egalitarian society, where there are neither exploited nor exploiters".

Lula's charisma and visionary ideals attracted many followers, and in 1990 he ran for president, an effort he would repeat in every subsequent election before finally winning in 2002 on his fourth attempt – and only after moderating his earlier leftist positions. It was a watershed moment in Brazilian history. For the first time ever, the country had a government on the left of the political spectrum and a president with first-hand knowledge of living in poverty. Initially, his victory alarmed investors and the ruling elite, who feared a leftist outsider running the economy aground. Yet, despite his anti-capitalist rhetoric of decades earlier, Lula ran one of the most fiscally responsible administrations in years, largely carrying on the work of his predecessor, President Fernando Henrique Cardoso. It was Cardoso, in fact, who as finance minister under Itamar Franco, introduced a new currency (the *real*) in 1994, which solved the problem of inflation and paved the way for Brazil's financial stability and future prosperity; it also catapulted Cardoso into the presidency in the next election.

Lula set to work immediately; he managed to repay the country's entire US$15 billion (£9.8 billion) debt to the IMF ahead of schedule in 2005, and set ambitious goals to help alleviate poverty and grow wealth for Brazilians across all social classes. On that count, Brazil has had remarkable success. An estimated 40 million Brazilians have been lifted out of poverty in the last decade, according to Maria Luiza Ribeiro Viotti, Brazil's permanent representative to the United Nations. The innovative *Bolsa Família* (Family Allowance) program deserves much of the credit. An anti-poverty scheme provides conditional cash transfers to Brazil's poorest families, providing a stipend per child attending school (maximum of three children). In order to receive the funds (generally sent to the female head of household), the children must stay in school and receive vaccinations. Thus, the program not only puts food on the table, but also improves access to education and healthcare. In 2012, it reached more than 13 million families, according to Brazil's *Ministério do Desenvolvimento Social e Combate à Fome* (Ministry of Social Development and Fight Against Hunger).

Brazil's foreign policy also expanded under Lula, as he forged closer ties with both Latin neighbours and distant allies. In the eight years of his presidency, bilateral trade soared to US$25 billion (£16.4), Brazil opened more than a dozen new embassies across South America and President Lula visited over 80 countries on state visits. He also helped give a greater voice to developing countries in emphasizing the key role G20 countries (the world's 20 major economies) would play in the global economy and in

RIGHT An indigenous boy in traditional costume consisting of brightly coloured feathers and black and red patterns painted on his cheeks.

PREVIOUS PAGE The Cristo Redentor (Christ the Redeemer) statue in Rio de Janeiro, at the peak of the Corcovado mountain. Constructed from 1926–1931, the 635 ton monument is possibly the most iconic image of Brazil that there is.

solving situations such as the global financial crisis of 2007–08.

Despite setbacks during Lula's presidency, which included a wave of scandals that saw a number of his PT party members resign in disgrace, the president was never implicated directly in any of the dealings, and he left office with stratospheric popularity ratings.

Lula's handpicked successor and fellow party member, Dilma Rousseff, was elected in 2010, becoming Brazil's first female head of state in history. Her unique background is no less extraordinary than Lula's. Though born to a privileged upper middle-class family, Rousseff decided to forego a university education and plunged straight into the world of activism after she finished high school in 1964. She joined a Marxist guerrilla group, and was arrested in São Paulo in 1970, where she was held in prison for almost three years and tortured. After her release, she resumed her studies in economics and followed a more conventional route through politics. Her rise through the ranks was meteoric: she was named Lula's minister of energy in 2002, and went on to become his chief of staff in 2005, where she remained until 2010 before stepping down to run for president.

Though Rousseff ran the country on the same socially progressive policies as Lula, once in office, she embraced a more "pragmatic capitalism". She has favoured the dismantling of some of Brazil's state-run industries, including airports, and invests heavily in entrepreneurship, wanting to build on the country's roots – Brazil has become one of the world's most entrepreneurial countries, with one in four adults self-employed in some capacity, according to a report from the World Bank. Rousseff has also tackled corruption, long entrenched in Brazilian politics. During her first year in office, six of her government ministers lost their positions due to their involvement in

corruption scandals. A tough, no-nonsense approach has boosted her approval ratings, which stood at over 70 per cent after her first year in office. Perhaps not surprisingly, in 2012 she was ranked the third most powerful woman in the world by *Forbes Magazine* – after Chancellor of Germany Angela Merkel and US Secretary of State Hillary Clinton.

Challenges ahead include investment in much-needed infrastructure. According to the World Economic Forum, Brazil's quality of physical infrastructure ranks 104th worldwide. Only 14 per cent of the roads are paved. To meet these needs, Rousseff has announced plans for competitive auctions to allow private contractors to bid for projects – including paving roads and building railways. She expects US$66 billion (£43.2) of investment over the coming years. Other plans include upgrading the country's mobile telecommunication networks, spurring small business creation by making it easier and faster for start-ups and simplifying Brazil's byzantine tax system. In social spending, Rousseff aims to open thousands of day-care centres for lower- to middle-class families and to continue the *Bolsa Família* program started up by her predecessor. She has also announced a program entitled Science Without Borders, which aims to send 100,000 Brazilians to study in the world's best universities by 2015.

PEOPLE & DIVERSITY

Brazil is one of the world's great melting pots. Brazilians can be of any colour and heritage, and hail from the most far-flung regions of the globe. Early Brazilians were a mix of Portuguese, African and Amerindian ancestry, while the late nineteenth and early twentieth centuries brought even more diversity as immigrants flooded into the country.

A look at famous Brazilians of past and present reveals an astonishing variety of ethnic backgrounds. There was Juscelino Kubitschek (1902–76), the president who spearheaded the creation of Brasília, of Czech and Roma descent; and supermodel Gisele Bündchen (1980–), whose Caucasian features and surname underscore her German-Brazilian roots. Fernando Haddad (1963–), the mayor of São Paulo and former minister of education in the cabinet of President Dilma Rousseff, is of Lebanese and Syrian origin. Ruy Ohtake (1938–), one of Brazil's most famous living architects, is the son of Tomie Ohtake (1913–) – herself a famous artist, who immigrated from Japan. The artist Candido Portinari (1903–62), a key figure of the Neorealist movement, was the son of Italian immigrants.

A journey around the country provides a window into the many facets of the Brazilian identity. The Northeast is home to some of Brazil's earliest settlements and the heart of Afro-Brazilian culture. In Salvador, heavy African-style drumbeats echo around the walls of the historic centre, while the scent of palm oil- and coconut flavoured seafood dishes (such as the seafood stew *moqueca*) linger in the air. In the streets, young kids practise high kicks and dance-like parries in the acrobatic game of *capoeira* – a martial art invented long ago by African slaves. By nightfall the devoted head for richly decorated worship halls, called *terreiros*, to participate in the polytheistic West African religion of *Candomblé*.

Meanwhile in the far South, Africa seems a world away from the European-style villages and their blonde-haired inhabitants. Blumenau embraces its German roots with huge folk festivals (including a massive *Oktoberfest*), old-world restaurants and microbrew-loving culture. In nearby Pomerode, German is still spoken by many of the town's residents.

The state of Rio Grande do Sul, with its cooler climate and dry, mountainous landscape, proved an excellent wine-growing region. In the nineteenth century, Italian immigrants planted many of the vineyards that flourish in the soil outside the town of Bento Gonçalves. This is the heart of Brazil's wine country; dozens of wineries here produce more than 12 million bottles a year. Gramado is perhaps the state's most European-style resort, with its alpine chalets and manicured streets sprinkled with fondue restaurants, German bakeries and boutiques specializing in gourmet chocolates and intricate glasswork.

In the hinterlands of Brazil's southernmost state, Rio Grande do Sul, lies the country's thriving *gaúcho* (cowboy) culture. Huge cattle ranches stretch across the *pampas* (grassy plains), while in its towns and cities old-timers in wide-brimmed hats hunker down over sizzling plates of *churrasco* (grilled steak), the favourite food of the South. Coffee plays second fiddle to *chimarrão*, the distinctive green-hued tea made from the yerba mate plant, served in these parts in a hollow calabash gourd with a metal straw.

In the Amazon, small and large cities are home to *mestiços* — persons of mixed race, often of Amerindian and European or African heritage. Deeper in the rainforest are Brazil's indigenous tribes, some 200 in all, with isolated communities that have not made contact with outside civilisation still living traditional lifestyles far removed from the modern world.

Brazil's massive cities unite these disparate elements of Brazilian culture and creed. São Paulo, the largest city of South America, is home to myriad immigrant communities, including the world's largest Japanese community outside of Japan itself. The neighbourhood of Liberdade is packed with traditional Japanese eateries and storefronts, while more recent immigrants from China and Korea contribute to the city's ever-evolving ethnic landscape. In São Paulo, there are also more people of Italian descent than any other city outside of Italy. The traditional Italian enclave of Bela Vista is famous for its Italian trattorias and delis — its deep-dish pizza is world-class. People of Arabic and Jewish descent, Latin Americans from other countries and many other nationalities add to the city's dynamism, as do migrants from all other parts of Brazil.

CULTURAL BEAT

Ethnic diversity has played no small role in Brazil's favourite traditions and celebrations. *Carnaval*, the nation's biggest and best-known festival, was brought over to the New World by the Portuguese, though in a much tamer fashion. Until the end of the nineteenth century, it was a mostly upper-class affair, consisting of masked balls and polka music. It acquired its present-day spirit of revelry when Afro-Brazilians began holding their own lively street parties, introducing African-style drumming and big brass bands. Indigenous elements — elaborate feather headdresses and body paint — are essential to the grand parades.

The origins of the festival are shrouded in mystery. *Carnaval* almost certainly originated from a pagan spring festival before being adopted into the Catholic calendar. The word *carnaval* itself may derive from the Latin *carne vale*, meaning "goodbye, meat", owing to the 40 days of abstinence from meat and other worldly pleasures that Lent entails. To compensate for the deprivation ahead, Brazilians rack up a few sins in advance at wild parties in honour of the mythic King Momo.

During *carnaval*, the whole country comes to a standstill (indeed most people take the whole week off work), with live music, street parades and all-night revelry happening everywhere in Brazil. Those wishing to escape the mayhem head out of town, typically to seaside resorts, for a slightly more sedate — though still festive — experience.

A pivotal element of *carnaval* is its soundtrack, which takes a wide variety of forms and provides a showcase for many great performers. Brazilians are naturally proud of their musical heritage, which ranks among the richest in the world in terms of artistic talent and sheer diversity of style. Samba is the signature sound of Rio, heard during *carnaval* and at all other times of year. It originated in a poor neighbourhood of migrants from Bahia, who incorporated African sounds and other elements (polkas; *maxixes*, which are akin to the tango; and *batuques*, a melodic music from Cape Verde). Though samba has never been out of fashion, in the last 15 years it has experienced an extraordinary renaissance, with the opening of numerous dancehalls in Rio's Lapa district.

Rio was also the birthplace of bossa nova, a melodic style of music with jazzy undertones that brought fame to the likes of Antônio Carlos Jobim, Vinícius de Moraes and João Gilberto, among many others. Bossa Nova hits such as "The Girl From Ipanema" became classics as international stars such as Frank Sinatra, Ella Fitzgerald and Stan Getz introduced new audiences to the distinctive Brazilian beat.

The Brazilian sound stretches across many genres, including pop, rock, funk, folk, hip hop and even metal. Perhaps because of the language barrier, many Brazilian musicians have not achieved as much fame abroad as the early bossa nova singers. But there are scores of great musicians and bands with millions of devoted followers within Brazil. Legends of the last 40 years include Jorge Ben Jor, who

LEFT An elaborately costumed dancer in the Rio *carnaval*.

BELOW Footballers Neymar (left) and his teammate Lucas dance in celebration after scoring in a friendly match against China, 2012. Neymar has been tipped as the next big thing in Brazilian football, and has been praised by Pelé for his skill.

celebrated Brazil's musical roots in albums such as *África Brasil* (1976), and Chico Buarque, the son of academic Sérgio Buarque de Holanda, and widely considered to be the nation's finest songwriter. Gilberto Gil wrote scores of hits prior to serving as Brazil's minister of culture from 2003–08 (and he was not averse to pulling out a guitar and breaking into song after a meeting at the World Economic Forum in Davos either). Music seems to be in the blood of many Brazilians, especially the singers of today, who carry on family traditions. Just a few top names include electro-pop singer Bebel Gilberto, daughter of João Gilberto; Maria Rita, daughter of Elis Regina – one of Brazil's all-time greats; Mart'nália, daughter of sambista Martinho da Vila; and Diogo Nogueira, son of singer João Nogueira.

Brazil's cultural dynamism extends far beyond the nation's concert halls and *escolas de samba* (samba schools), however. In the realm of sport, the country has long dominated the beautiful game, with some of the finest footballers who have ever lived, including Pelé, Ronaldo, Ronaldinho and current star Neymar. Every Brazilian has a favourite team – and in cities like Rio, with four major club teams, the rivalry is intense – but nothing quite compares to the crackling electricity in the air when the *Seleção Brasileira* (National Team) takes to the field. The football-mad nation has finally fulfilled a long-time dream: bringing the World Cup back to Brazil. Twelve different cities will host the 2014 matches, and the country has spent an unprecedented US$13.7 billion (£8.8 billion) in preparation for the event.

While not quite as popular as football, Brazilian cinema has grown tremendously in the last 30 years – since creative expression finally returned after the stifling days of the military dictatorship (1964–85).

Hard-hitting films such as Walter Salles's *Central Station* (1998) and Fernando Meirelles's *City of God* (2002) introduced viewers to the harsh reality of life among Brazil's poorest communities. Today's top directors build on the earlier traditions of *cinema novo* (new cinema), a 1960s movement that shone a spotlight on the country's enormous social problems.

ART & ARCHITECTURE

Brazil's art and architecture were strongly influenced by European influences throughout much of the nation's history. Early artistic treasures showcase works of the Portuguese baroque, a style of free ornamentation and extravagant forms visible in scores of lavish, gold-filled churches, eighteenth-century manor houses and even palaces around Brazil. Half a dozen historic town centres have been named UNESCO World Heritage Sites, including Salvador in Bahia, Olinda in Pernambuco and São Luis in the far northern state of Maranhão. The discovery of gold in 1696 in present-day Minas Gerais, and the riches that subsequently flowed through its newly formed towns, led to the creation of architecturally lavish cities such as Ouro Preto, another UNESCO-listed site and one of the finest colonial towns in the Americas. It has 23 historic churches, including the stunning São Francisco de Assis, designed by the celebrated architect and sculptor Antônio Francisco Lisboa in 1774.

In the nineteenth century, the Neoclassical style came to dominate Brazil, thanks in large part to the transfer of the entire Portuguese royal court to the New World. King Dom João VI helped remodel Rio de Janeiro, which in the early 1800s was a humble colonial town. He organized the creation of the

French Artistic Mission that brought great painters and architects to the new capital of a united Portugal-Brazil empire, and bequeathed on the city a love of European culture that would continue into the 1900s.

The birth of a uniquely Brazilian style would arrive with twentieth-century Modernism. A seminal event for Brazil's visual artists was Modern Art Week, held in São Paulo in 1922. The arts festival, which featured painting and sculpture, as well as literature, poetry and music, proved controversial as young Modernists broke away from academic styles, presenting works that were considered radical for the time. Some poets and musicians were even booed off the stage. Despite the initial cold reception, the show would help launch the careers of several important artists, including Tarsila do Amaral, Anita Catarina Malfatti, Cândido Portinari and Emiliano Di Cavalcanti, who are among Brazil's most important twentieth-century painters. It also established São Paulo as the seat of Brazil's Modern Art movement, and marked a definitive rupture with the past and the dawn of something new.

Another key event in the Modern Art movement in Brazil was the publication of the *Manifesto Antropófago* (Cannibal Manifesto) by the poet and polemicist Oswald de Andrade in 1928. In his essay he describes the Brazilian appetite for "cannibalizing" other cultures, then digesting and creating something anew from it. The idea later gained traction under the *Tropicalistas* – a movement in music, visual arts and theatre that emerged in the 1960s. In recordings of the time, Caetano Veloso and Gilberto Gil incorporated a wide range of musical influences from abroad (psychedelic rock, pop, funk), which they melded

ABOVE Children play football in São Paulo, 2010. From a young age, Brazilians get involved in and cultivate a passion for the beautiful game.

LEFT The *gruta do lago azul* (blue lake grotto) in Bonito, Mato Grosso do Sul. Discovered in 1924 by one of the local Tereno indigenous tribe, the luminous effect of the water is created by shafts of sunlight from outside. In 1992, a Franco-Brazilian expedition discovered thousands of prehistoric animal bones on the lake floor.

ABOVE The Cathedral of Brasília by Oscar Niemeyer. Built as part of the construction of the county's new capital city, the structure was completed in 1960, but was not officially opened until 1970. Only the 16 concrete columns and stained glass roof are visible above ground, surrounded by a pool of water, which act as a coolant to the space inside.

with Brazilian styles (samba, bossa nova) to create a wildly eclectic sound.

Modernism has played an even bigger role in shaping Brazilian architecture. Oscar Niemeyer (1907–2012) became a leading figure in a group of young Modernists who would bring bold ideas to the world of urban design. He created striking exterior forms, with unusual curves and a lilting ethereal beauty, evident in works such as the Contemporary Art Museum in the city of Niterói, Rio de Janeiro; Pampulha architectural complex in Belo Horizonte and the auditorium in Ibirapuera Park, São Paulo. Niemeyer collaborated with urban planner Lúcio Costa (1902–98) and landscape architect Roberto Burle Marx (1909–94) on the design of Brasília, a city representing a utopian vision of the future, with grand, sculptural architecture with a harmonious aesthetic. Some of his most famous designs were for buildings in the new capital, including the presidential palace Palácio do Planalto, the Catedral Metropolitana and the Congresso Nacional do Brasil. He left behind a formidable body of work and influenced several generations of architects.

Brazilian design continues to evolve, with new artists, architects and urban planners at the fore. Tunga, one of Brazil's top living artists, combines constructivist and surrealist elements in emotive sculptural works. Influenced by the avant-garde artist Hélio Oiticica, Ernesto Neto creates massive labyrinth-like installations that often bring the viewer inside. Colourful urban artists such as Otavio and Gustavo Pandolfo (who go by the name Os Gêmeos) have been adding their oversized, intricate murals to street scenes in São Paulo and other cities, while photographer Sebastião Salgado has earned worldwide fame for his evocative landscapes and gripping portraits. Major art fairs in both Rio de Janeiro and São Paulo – which hosts the second oldest biennial in the world after the Venice Biennale – provide a platform for rising stars.

NATURAL LANDSCAPE

Blessed with tropical rainforest, lush wetland, mountain ranges and over 7,500 km (4,660 miles) of sparkling coastline, Brazil has a wide array of natural treasures. Spreading across half of Brazil, the vast Amazon rainforest is the most species-rich tropical rainforest on earth, where pink river dolphins, caiman, 100 kg (220 lb) fish and the ubiquitous piranha rule the rivers, and a thick canopy hides hundreds of bird species, including harpy eagles, toucans, macaws and parrots. There are also more mammal species here than anywhere else in the world – from the powerful and stealthy jaguar to the pencil-long pygmy marmoset, which at 100 g (3.5 oz) is the world's smallest monkey. Despite its renown, the Amazon still retains many of its secrets. Major tributaries have yet to be explored, thousands of species remain unclassified and dozens of human communities have thus far avoided contact with the outside world.

Another biodiversity hotspot is the Pantanal, an immense area of wetland, savannah and forest located south of the Amazon. Home to many of the same animal species found in the Amazon, the planet's largest tropical wetland ecosystem is a major draw for wildlife watching. Along much of the east coast stretches remnants of the Atlantic rainforest, home to a high number of endemic species. Several islands are found in this rapidly disappearing ecosystem, including the Fernando de Noronha archipelago in the Northeast and Ilha Grande in the Southeast.

The interior is home to several mountainous regions containing *chapada* – dramatic landscapes of canyons, plateaux, caves, waterfalls and mountain rivers. Stretching between Argentina and Brazil, the mighty Iguazu Falls is one of the world's great spectacles – not only for its sheer power, but also because of the surrounding rare and endangered species of flora and fauna.

NATURAL RESOURCES & THE FUTURE OF BRAZIL

Brazil's wealth has long been connected to its wealth of natural resources, from brasilwood and sugarcane of the early colonial period to biofuel and oil of more recent years. Today, Brazil has diversified its economy, with trade partners across the globe. It has booming agricultural and industrial sectors extending to automobile and aircraft production, steel, petrochemicals and computers. How the country manages resources and balances sustainability versus profit will play a pivotal role in its future.

As Brazil prepares to host the 2014 World Cup and the 2016 Summer Olympics the future has never looked brighter. Substantial investment in infrastructure, healthcare and education aim to improve the quality of life for the country's poorest, while newly discovered oil reserves, a rock-solid currency and a fiscally prudent administration all provide the fuel to keep the economic pistons firing – which are just a few of the reasons why the Economist Intelligence Unit (EIU) predicts that by 2020 Brazil's economy will have outgrow any in Europe, making it the world's fifth largest global economy.

HISTORY AND EARLY DEVELOPMENT

The first inhabitants of the Americas probably arrived in waves from about 12,000 to 8000 BC, travelling from Siberia across the ancient Bering land bridge that once connected Asia and North America. Over the following millennia, they spread southward, settling in every corner of the Americas and throughout Brazil. By the time the Europeans arrived there were probably between two and six million indigenous people, representing more than 100 separate language groups, spread across the vast rainforests and seemingly endless coastlines of present-day Brazil.

Their fate, and that of the continent itself, changed forever when Portuguese explorer Pedro Álvares Cabral first set foot on South American soil in 1500, claiming the land for the Portuguese crown. Although the discovery was initially greeted with indifference (neither gold, spices, nor precious gems accompanied the return voyage), Portuguese merchants soon discovered the commercial value of so-called brazilwood, a native timber used to manufacture a luxurious crimson dye.

Settlers arrived to work the land, with Portuguese King João III granting each of the 14 captaincies in 1531 to minor gentry, who would oversee the colony's development and protection from rival European powers. Within a generation, however, the easily accessible brazilwood stocks were almost exhausted, and the colonists set their sights on sugarcane, a lucrative industry fuelled by Europe's sweet tooth. The only problem: a bigger labour force was needed.

Like Spain and other European empires of the time, Portugal embraced the diabolical practice of raiding villages in Africa and transporting its human cargo to the New World. Open-air slave markets in Salvador and Rio flourished by the turn of the seventeenth century, fuelled by the boom in the sugarcane industry.

From the 1550s until slavery was finally abolished in the late 1800s, over three million slaves were brought to Brazil.

On the plantations, male slaves toiled away at 17-hour shifts in the blazing tropical heat, while their female counterparts were used to satisfy the carnal needs of their white masters. Sexual relations were common, leading to cohabitation and sometimes marriage between male colonizers and their female slaves. For better or worse, this early mixing of races played a pivotal role in creating Brazil's multiracial society.

Abhorrent working and living conditions (with 200 or more slaves packed into a squalid bunkhouse) led to strong resistance. Some escaped to form *quilombos*, or communities of runaway slaves hidden across the countryside. One famous *quilombo*, Palmares, had as many as 20,000 inhabitants and lasted almost a century before its annihilation by *bandeirantes* (slave hunters and explorers) in the 1690s.

At the turn of the eighteenth century, news spread of the discovery of gold in the interior, and soon the rush was on. Boomtowns sprang up practically overnight as prospectors from Portugal, slaves brought from Africa and migrants from the northeast all converged on the mountain valleys of present-day Minas Gerais. In a formerly barren part of the country the population exploded (from 30,000 inhabitants in 1710 to 500,000 by 1800). Gold and later diamonds helped bankroll lavish baroque churches across the country, and Rio de Janeiro, the nearest port city to the goldfields, replaced Salvador as the capital of Brazil.

During the gold rush, Rio de Janeiro grew substantially but saw even greater transformations in the following century, thanks to one diminutive Frenchman by the name of Napoleon Bonaparte. In

1807, as Napoleon's troops invaded Portugal, the Portuguese Royal Court and its retinue of 15,000 boarded ships and fled to Brazil. The newly installed Prince Regent (later Dom João VI) became the first European monarch to set foot in the New World. Yet, far from viewing Brazil as a temporary sanctuary he fell under the spell of the colonial capital and showered it with wealth. He created a naval academy, a school of medicine, a printing house, a fine arts academy, the nation's first bank and botanical gardens that are still a major landmark today. European artists and artisans brought bold new architecture to the city, while the economy flourished amid the opening of Brazil's ports to international trade. Even after Napoleon's defeat at Waterloo in 1815, Dom João VI showed little interest in leaving Brazil. In fact, the following year, he elevated the country's status by declaring Rio the capital of the United Kingdom of Portugal, Brazil and the Algarves.

The King finally returned to Portugal in 1821, leaving his son Pedro in Brazil as prince regent. Back in Lisbon, the Portuguese parliament put pressure on Dom João VI to return its colonial status. When word reached Pedro back in Brazil, according to legend he pulled out his sword, declaring "*Independencia ou morte!*" (independence or death!). Portugal had little desire to wage a costly war, and so Brazil became independent without a shot being fired. Unfortunately, the newly crowned Emperor of Brazil, Pedro I, proved an incompetent ruler, and was forced to abdicate in 1831, leaving the throne to his five-year-old son, Pedro II.

Pedro II proved a far more capable monarch, and over his 50-year reign, he guided Brazil through a period of growth and prosperity. By the 1850s, regular passenger ships connected Rio with both London and Paris, while a telegraph service and gas streetlights made it one of South America's most modern cities. By 1860, it was also the largest, with 250,000 inhabitants. Railways spread across Brazil, and new industries boomed – particularly coffee production and rubber plantations. Slave trafficking was banned in 1850, but it wasn't until 1888 that slavery was finally abolished. For many of the 800,000 newly freed slaves, life didn't immediately improve. Thousands were cast out into the streets, without a safety net to help them adjust to a startling new reality. The majority sought refuge in urban centres, creating some of the country's first *favelas*, or slums.

Shortly after the end of slavery, the monarchy was toppled in a coup d'état that sent an elderly Pedro II and his family into exile. The new Brazilian Republic adopted a constitution modelled on that of the US, although the military and the increasingly powerful coffee barons essentially ruled behind the scenes. For most Brazilians, little ultimately changed as the country went from empire to republic.

Once slavery was abolished, Brazil instigated an open-door policy to attract new immigrants, both to replace the loss of labour and to whiten the country's ethnic mix. Millions heeded the call, coming predominantly from Italy, Portugal, Spain, Germany and Japan. All added to Brazil's growing diversity and fuelled the explosive growth in cities, especially São Paulo and Rio. Between 1890 and 1930, the population grew by more than 160 per cent. The economy boomed, with investment in manufacturing, textiles, agriculture and mineral exports.

The year 1930 marked the beginning of an autocratic era in Brazilian politics. Backed by the newly formed Liberal Alliance party, Getúlio Vargas unsuccessfully ran for president in 1930. No matter, his allies helped organize street protests and, as violence

spread from south to north, the military stepped in and deposed democratically elected Júlio Prestes before handing the reins to Vargas. An admirer of Italy's Benito Mussolini, Vargas announced the formation of the *Estado Novo* (New State) in 1937. He banned political parties, imprisoned opponents and censored the press. Yet for all this, Vargas had many supporters, particularly among the working class. Although strikes were outlawed, he established labour laws (including a minimum wage and workers' benefits) that were progressive for their time. In the process, he earned himself the nickname o *pai dos pobres* (the father of the poor).

After World War II, Vargas was forced to step down, although he re-entered politics in 1951, winning the presidential election – this time democratically. But his tenure was marred by corruption. With mounting pressure from the military, Vargas realized his days in office would soon come to an end. Rather than retire from the limelight, on 24 August 1954, he penned a suicide note and shot himself in the heart. He was dead at the age of 72, leaving behind a wife and five children.

Juscelino Kubitschek filled the power vacuum left by Vargas. JK – as he was popularly known – had grand ambitions when he took office, promising among other things "fifty years' progress in five". In some ways he delivered, laying the foundation for a modern, prosperous economy with the expansion of heavy industry and large-scale production. His greatest achievement though was the building of Brasília, carving a grandly designed city – completed in just four years – in a barren expanse of savannah. Unfortunately, JK had to borrow heavily to finance the project, and inflation surged under his administration – a feature that would dog Brazil's economy for the next 30 years.

Another election occurred in 1961, though it proved a fateful one. With fears of communism sweeping across the Americas, the military overthrew the left-leaning João Goulart in 1964. Power was handed over to General Humberto de Alencar Castelo Branco, the first of a series of military rulers to govern over the next 21 years. Although less brutal than the regimes of Argentina or Chile, the dictatorship in Brazil nevertheless banned political parties and exiled, jailed or murdered dissidents. Censorship was widespread. Oddly, the repression coincided with a continued boom, with the economy growing by an average of 10 per cent annually between the late 1960s and mid-1970s. It was also a time of spending on massive projects such as the Transamazônica highway (never fully completed) and Itaipu dam, which, at the time of its opening in 1984, was the largest hydroelectric dam ever built. At the same time, inflation exploded and the gulf between rich and poor grew ever wider.

By the late 1970s, the "economic miracle" came sputtering to an end amid widespread opposition to the regime. Following a cautious period of *abertura* (opening), civilian rule finally returned in the presidential election of 1985. Millions of Brazilians took to the streets, celebrating the end of military rule. Unfortunately, the festivities were short-lived – democratically elected Tancredo Neves died of peritonitis at the age of 75 before he could be sworn in. Civilian rule, however, was there to stay, and 21 years of dictatorship at last came to an end. Brazil still had enormous problems to contend with: runaway inflation, political corruption, extreme poverty and social inequality, along with exploding violence in its cities. It would take a former factory worker and union leader – an unlikely president by the name of Lula – to turn things around.

OPPOSITE Engraving depicting Portuguese explorer Pedro Álvares Cabral (c.1467–1520), who is regarded as having discovered Brazil. On April 22, 1500, his 13 ships arrived where today sits the state of Bahia. Originally the fleet had set sail from Lisbon on a mission to India, but historians dispute the version that Cabral's discovery of Brazil was accidental.

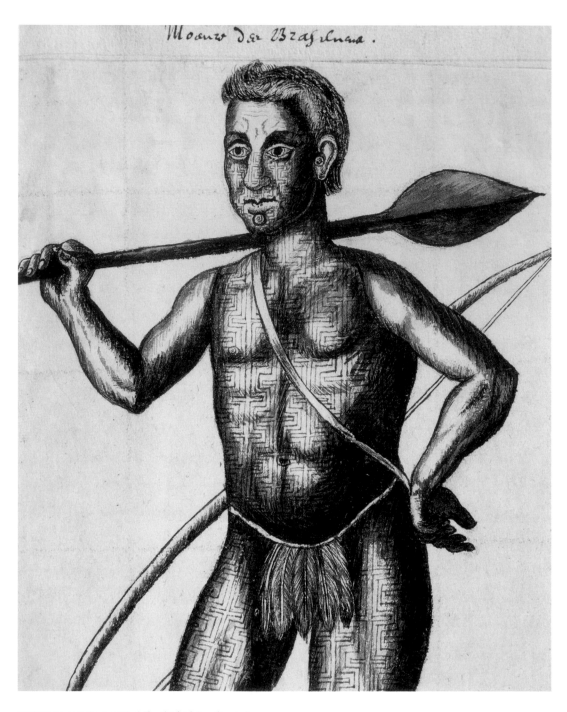

ABOVE Watercolour entitled *The chief of Brazilian Indians* (1633). Little is known of Brazil's first inhabitants, but experts estimate that when Portuguese explorers arrived in 1500 there were between two and six million indigenous people, representing more than 100 separate language groups.

ACCURATISSIMA
BRASILIÆ
TABULA.
Amstelodami
Henricus Hondius excudit.

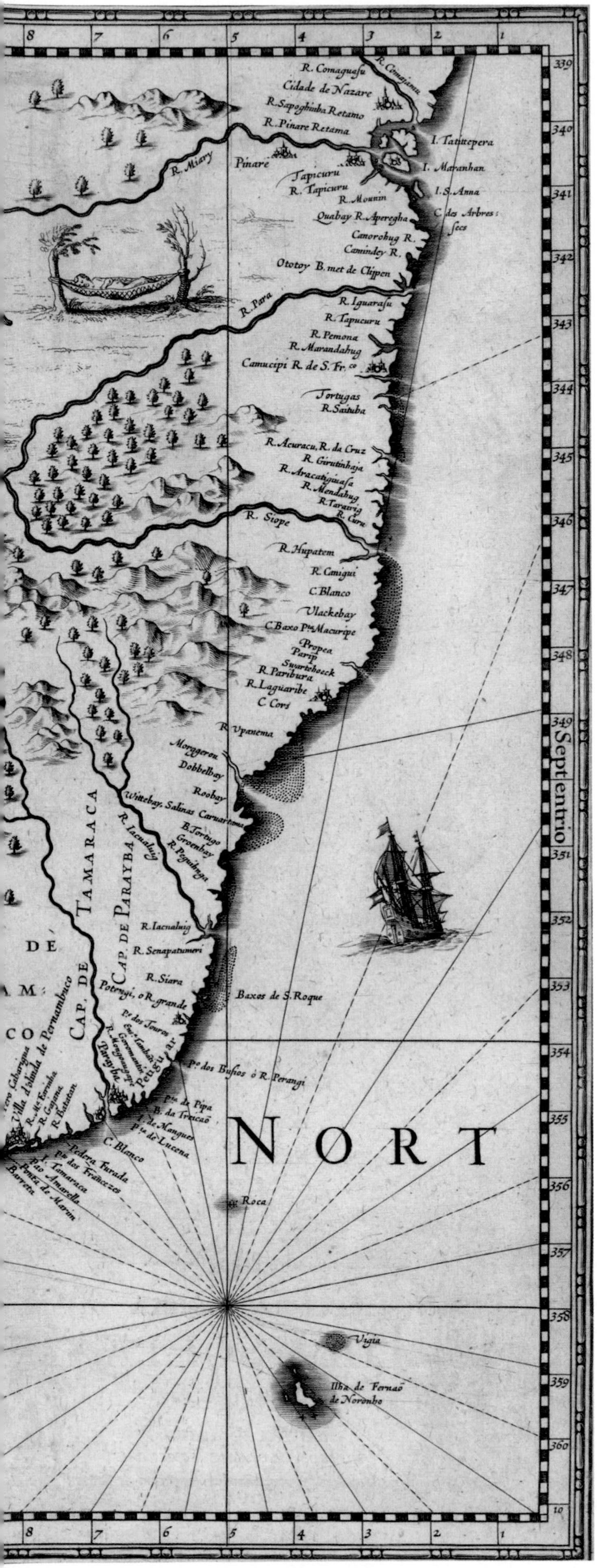
R. Comaguasu
Cidade de Nazare
R. Sapoghiuba Retamo
R. Pinare Retama
R. Miary
Pinare
Tapicuru
R. Tapicuru
I. Tatitepera
I. Maranhan
I. S. Anna
C des Arbres secs
Ototoy B. met de Clipen
R. Para
R. Iguarasu
R. Tapucuru
R. Pemona
R. Marandahug
Camucipi R. de S. Fr. co
Tortugas
R. Saituba
R. Siope
R. Hupatem
R. Camigui
C. Blanco
Vlackebay
R. Laguaribe
C. Cors
R. Upanema
Morygeron
Dobbelbay
Roobay
B. Tortugo
TAMARACA
CAP. DE PARAYBA
R. Iacualuig
R. Senapatumeri
R. Siara
Potengi, o R. grande
Baxos de S. Roque
CAP. DE
DE
CO
C. Blanco
Villa d'olinda de Pernambuco
NORT
Roca
Vigia
Ilha de Fernaõ de Noronho
Septentrio

LEFT An early map of Brazil by engraver, cartographer and publisher Hendrik Hondius II that shows the administrative division of Brazil in 1630, reflecting the system set up by the Portuguese Crown in 1534. The so-called "hereditary captaincies" were huge stretches of land delivered to Portuguese nobleman and governed independently until 1549, when a central government was established in Salvador. In 1821, the captaincies were replaced with provinces.

ABOVE A view of Recife, capital of the state of Pernambuco, c.1850. Having been the most prosperous Brazilian captaincy during the sixteenth and seventeenth centuries due to the success of sugarcane plantation and a brief period under Dutch administration, Pernambuco is today the tenth largest economy in Brazil.

TOP This handcoloured engraving shows African slaves washing for alluvial gold, watched over by a slave master brandishing a whip (1814). The discovery of the precious metal at the turn of the eighteenth century, in areas miles away from the coastline, contributed to the decline of sugarcane and created a new source of wealth in colonial Brazil.

ABOVE An illustration from *Les Indes Orientales et Occidentales, et Autres Lieux* by Romeyn de Hooghe shows a sugarcane processing mill in Brazil, c.1700. Following the decline of brazilwood (or pau-brasil) in the sixteenth century, sugarcane became the basis of Brazilian economy for almost 200 years, being produced mainly in Pernambuco, Bahia and São Paulo.

ABOVE Dance of the Ticuna indigenous tribe, c.1870. Today, around 30,000 Ticuna live near the borders of Brazil, Peru and Colombia. The tribe's first contact with non-indigenous people happened in the late seventeenth century, when Spanish Jesuits arriving from Peru founded missionary villages on the shores of the Solimões River.

ABOVE The French painter Jean-Baptiste Debret (1768–1848) lived in Brazil for 15 years, when he produced a large number of images depicting everyday life in the country. After his return to Paris, in 1831, he published a series of volumes called *A Picturesque and Historic Voyage to Brazil,* with engravings such as *Wild Dance in São José Mission* (1839).

Négresse de Bahia.

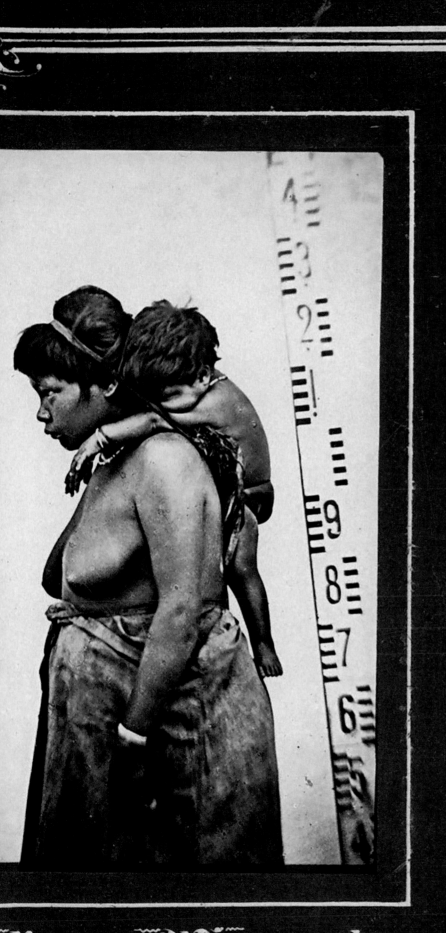

dienne-Botocudo.

Marc Fer

LEFT Portrait of a Brazilian woman from Bahia and an indigenous mother and child from the Botocudo tribe, c.1882. Slavery began in Brazil's early colonial years and lasted for more than 300 years. Initially indigenous men and women were made slaves, but the main workforce throughout the colonial period consisted of those captured and brought from West Africa.

OPPOSITE The fourth child of Dom João VI and Dona Carlota Joaquina became heir to the Portuguese throne after the death of his elder brother, Francisco António, in 1801. Dom Pedro I (1798–1834) became the first Emperor of Brazil after he declared independence in 1822, and was named King Dom Pedro IV of Portugal in 1826.

TOP Brazilian slave traders inspect a group of Africans shipped into the country for sale. From the 1550s until slavery was abolished in 1888, over three million slaves were brought to Brazil. Abhorrent living and working conditions led to strong resistance, with some slaves escaping to form independent communities, or *quilombos*.

ABOVE As Napoleon's troops invaded Portugal in 1807, the Portuguese royal court and its retinue of 15,000 boarded ships and fled to Brazil. The newly installed Prince Regent, Dom João VI, was proclaimed Emperor of Brazil and Portugal in Rio de Janeiro in 1816.

ABOVE Dom João VI returned to Portugal in 1821, leaving his son Pedro in Brazil. According to legend, on September 7, 1822, when the Prince received news that the Portuguese parliament had increased pressure to return the new land to its colonial status, he pulled out his sword and declared "*Independência ou morte!*" (Independence or death).

LEFT Jean-Baptiste Debret was Dom João VI's favourite painter in Rio de Janeiro. Here, he portrays the landing of Princess Maria Leopoldina of Austria (1797–1826) in 1817, who came to Brazil to marry Pedro of Bragança (the future Dom Pedro I), heir to the Portuguese throne. Debret published a series of three volumes of engravings about Brazil but the work did not enjoy commercial success.

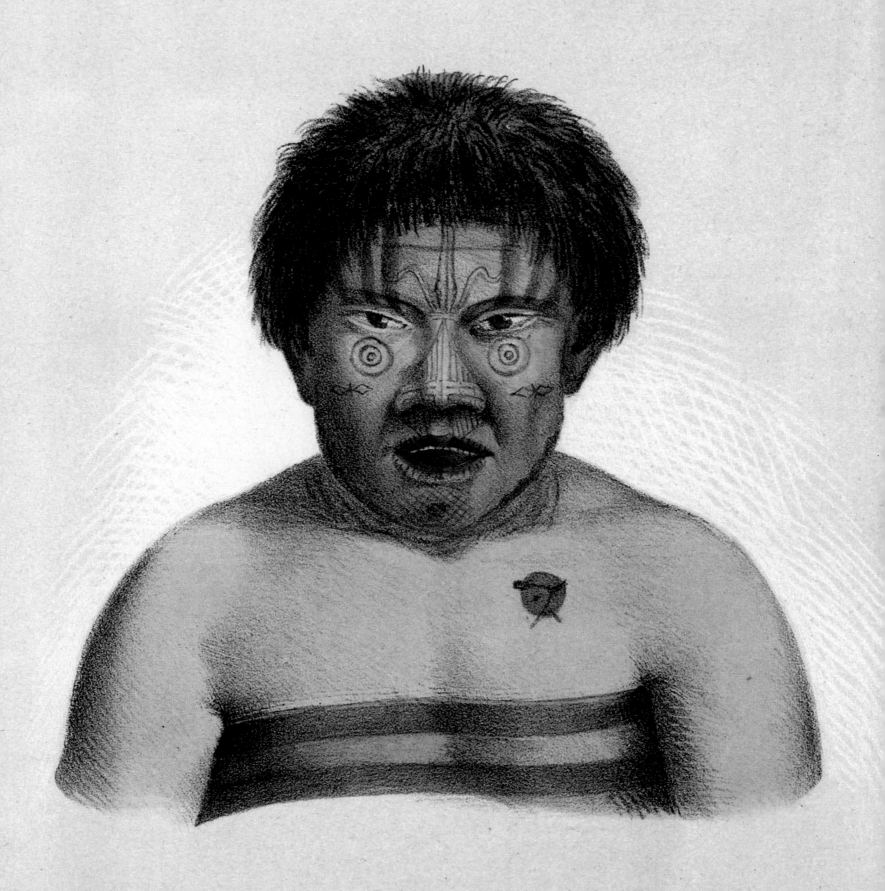

PREVIOUS A lithograph of two members of the Guaycuru tribe from Brazil, Paraguay or Argentina from *Expedition in the Central Parts of South America* by Francis de Castelnau (1812–80), published in Paris in 1852. The book is an account of the French government's scientific expedition led by Francis de Castelnau between 1843 and 1847. The party travelled across South America to La Paz, in Bolivia.

RIGHT Dom Pedro II (1825–91). The son of Dom Pedro I was only 5 years old when his father was forced to abdicate. At 14, he was declared of age and a year later, he was crowned. Over his 58-year reign, Dom Pedro II guided Brazil through a period of growth and prosperity. Despite his popularity, the Emperor was overthrown in 1889 by a group of republican military leaders.

ABOVE Illustration depicting the laying of the foundation stone of the Petrópolis Railway in 1852. This was the first of many railways built in Brazil under the rule of Dom Pedro II. Nicknamed "The Magnanimous", the Emperor is remembered for his strong sponsorship of culture, science and development.

ABOVE Engraving by Rico illustrates the ovation in Rio de Janeiro for Marshal Deodoro da Fonseca, leader of a military coup d'état that pacifically deposed Dom Pedro II and established Brazil as a republic, on November 15, 1889. On the same day, a provisional government was formed and Fonseca was named as the country's first president.

TOP RIGHT The first government of the Republic of the United States of Brazil, in 1889, with President Marshal Deodoro da Fonseca (1827–92) in the centre. A new constitution was developed and came into force in 1891, ratifying Marshal Fonseca's post. He would rule for another nine months before resigning in favour of his vice-president, Floriano Peixoto.

BOTTOM RIGHT Oil on canvas by Francisco Tirone depicts the constitutional oath of Princess Isabel of Bragança, first daughter of Dom Pedro II and heir to the Brazilian Crown, in 1860. She was Brazil's first female senator and served as regent on three separate occasions – the most well known in 1888, when she signed the *Lei Áurea*, a law emancipating all slaves in Brazil.

ABOVE An illustration of Rio de Janeiro city and harbour in the nineteenth century. Since 1763, the colonial capital underwent deep transformation after the arrival of Dom João VI in 1808. He created a naval academy, a school of medicine, an academy of fine arts and the nation's first bank.

OPPOSITE Founded by the Portuguese in 1565, Rio de Janeiro became a prosperous port for the gold and diamonds of Minas Gerais during the eighteenth century and grew even faster in the following years as the colonial capital. Near the port, streets such as Rua do Ouvidor attracted shoppers and traders. Rio would remain the political epicentre of Brazil until the inauguration of Brasília in 1960.

ABOVE Loading coffee on a plantation, c.1900–1920. Largely supported by the national government, coffee production generated unprecedented wealth in São Paulo, leading to its rapid modernisation and growth. The so-called coffee barons – big producers and exporters – had a crucial role in the establishment of the Republic in 1889 and continued to influence Brazilian politics until the 1920s.

ABOVE Coffee sun-drying in São Paulo, c.1900–1920. Introduced in Brazil in the early eighteenth century, coffee didn't become the country's main product of export until 100 years later, when the bean reached high prices in the world market. Coffee production developed mainly in the Paraíba Valley, between the states of Rio and São Paulo, expanding later to Paraná.

ABOVE Indigenous people and explorer in Amazonia, c.1920. The Amazon region, with its indigenous tribes and diverse wildlife, has fascinated both European and Brazilian explorers since the beginning of the colonization. In the seventeenth century the first Portuguese settled in the area, looking for gold and indigenous slaves. The rubber boom, between 1880 and 1910, put the region in the international spotlight forever.

LEFT A crowd of Italian immigrants and their descendants in the Brasital textiles factory, Salto, São Paulo State, c.1930. The end of slavery in Brazil and the coffee boom of the late nineteenth century contributed to an intense flux of European immigrants. Italians settled mostly in São Paulo and in Rio Grande do Sul.

ABOVE Born in Cuiabá, Mato Grosso, Gen. Eurico Gaspar Dutra (right) (1883–1974) was minister of war in Getúlio Vargas' government from 1936–45. Dutra was elected president in December 1945. His tenure was marked by pro-US policies that saw the ban of the Brazilian Communist Party and the rupture of relations with the Soviet Union.

TOP An admirer of Mussolini, Getúlio Vargas (1882–1954) came to power after a coup d'état in October 1930. On November 10, 1937, amid fears of a communist plan to depose him, President Vargas declared the *Estado Novo* (new state), which shut down congress and established an authoritarian nationalist constitution, lasting until 1945.

OPPOSITE A display at Museu da República in Rio shows the shirt worn by President Getúlio Vargas when he shot himself through the heart on August 24, 1954. Vargas had been re-elected democratically in 1951. Following accusations that his chief of guard had masterminded a plot to assassinate a political rival, Vargas faced increased pressure to resign, but instead decided to "leave life to enter history", as he said in his dramatic suicide note that was read aloud on national radio just two hours after the discovery of his body.

ABOVE The German-built LZ 127 Graf Zeppelin made its first visit to Brazil in 1930, departing from Friedrichshafen and stopping in Seville, Spain, and Recife, in Northeastern Brazil, before reaching Rio de Janeiro. A regular service of passengers and freight between Germany and the Brazilian capital operated between 1932 and 1937.

ABOVE Minas Gerais-born Juscelino Kubitschek (1902–76) (right) acclaimed by the crowd in Rio de Janeiro in 1956, when he took office as president, along with Vice-President João Goulart. Kubitschek promised to deliver "fifty years of progress in five" and laid the foundations for a modern, prosperous economy. His greatest achievement was the building of Brasília, construction of which began in 1956 and was completed in 1960.

TOP Ministry buildings under construction in the new Brazilian capital of Brasília, 1959. The idea of moving the capital from Rio to the Brazilian interior dates from the first republican constitution, in 1891, but it was only under Kubitschek that Brasília materialised.

ABOVE Workers from all over the country, especially
from the Northeast, were attracted by the building of the
new capital and became known as *candangos* (as above,
pictured in 1958). Many of them remained around Brasília
after its inauguration, leading to a demographic boom in
its first decades and the establishment of smaller and more
deprived towns around the city.

ABOVE Legislative buildings under construction in the new
Brazilian capital, 1960. The architect Lúcio Costa won a
public contest to become the city's urban planner, while the
acclaimed Oscar Niemeyer designed most of the public
buildings, such as these. Construction lasted 41 months.

LEFT A populist rhetoric and extravagant behaviour granted Jânio Quadros (1917-1992) a meteoric political career, which culminated with his election as president in 1960. He would, however, govern for only seven months. He resigned in August 1961, pressured by right-wing groups who labelled his policies as "communist", making way for his vice-president, João Goulart.

LEFT General Humberto Castelo Branco assumed power on April 15 1964, two weeks after a military coup ousted President João Goulart. Unlike other dictatorial regimes in South America, Brazil had five military rulers that were elected by Congress.

OPPOSITE Born in Rio Grande do Sul, left-leaning President João Goulart (or Jango, as he was known) had been minister of labour in Varga's administration and Vice-President during the Juscelino Kubitschek years. After almost three years in office, he was deposed by a military coup that was largely supported by the United States. He died in exile in 1976 in circumstances that still remain to be thoroughly investigated.

ABOVE General Ernesto Geisel (at the head of the table) presiding over his first cabinet meeting on March 25, 1974. The Brazilian economy grew an average of 10 per cent annually between the late 1960s and mid-1970s, under the military regime. General Geisel was president from 1974 to 1979, a period during which massive projects like the Transamazônica highway, the underground networks of São Paulo and Rio and the Itaipu dam were boosted.

OPPOSITE TOP The military government in Brazil banned political parties and exiled, jailed or murdered dissidents. In 1979, after years of campaigning from families, with the support of opposition leaders, the country's last military president, General João Figueiredo (pictured), signed the law that granted amnesty to those prosecuted.

OPPOSITE BELOW An estimated 1 million people gather in front of the Candelária Church in central Rio on April 10, 1984, to demand direct presidential elections after 20 years of military rule. Despite the massive popular approval, the *Diretas Já* (direct elections now) campaign failed to persuade congress, which voted for the continuation of the indirect system established by the military.

ABOVE One of the main leaders of the opposition during the military regime, Tancredo Neves (1910–85) (centre) was elected the first civil president of Brazil since 1961 on January 15, 1985. Celebrating victory with his wife, Risoleta, by his side, Neves would never take office. He fell ill on the eve of his oath and died on April 21, 1985.

ABOVE Brazilians followed with great interest and commotion the illness of President-elect Tancredo Neves, who was admitted to hospital one day before taking office, on March 14, 1985. Crowds gathered in vigil in front of Instituto do Coração in São Paulo, where he died on April 21, after being submitted to seven abdominal operations.

ABOVE An estimated 15,000 people rally in downtown Rio de Janeiro on August 14, 1992, demanding the impeachment of President Fernando Collor de Mello. A congressional panel investigated allegations of influence peddling and tax evasion against Paulo Cesar Farias, a businessman and close friend of the president who served as treasurer for Collor's 1989 election campaign.

TOP A former member of the ruling party during the military years, José Sarney took office as the president in March 1985, following the illness of president-elect Tancredo Neves. His administration was marked by the failed *Plano Cruzado*, the first of a series of shock measures intended to curb hyperinflation.

ABOVE The heir of one of the most influential political dynasties in Brazil's Northeast, Fernando Collor de Mello came to power as the first directly elected president in almost 30 years. But allegations of corruption spread by his own brother led to a national popular movement demanding his impeachment, a process that he avoided by resigning in 1992.

LEFT An employee at a supermarket puts up new price signs in August 1993, as Brazil changes its currency from the cruzeiro to cruzeiro real, the first step in a new plan devised to control the country's hyperinflation. At this stage, inflation was running at a rate of 32 per cent each month.

ABOVE A long-standing centre-left leader, Fernando Henrique Cardoso took office in January 1995 after a successful tenure as President Itamar Franco's minister of finance, when he introduced measures that managed to control the hyperinflation that had haunted Brazilians for many decades, paving the way to a more economically stable country.

ABOVE Luiz Inácio Lula da Silva (1945–) was the seventh child of illiterate peasants from Pernambuco. Having received little formal education, Lula (as he became known) began working in a factory at the age of 14. In 1978, he became head of the powerful Steel Workers' Union, initiating a political career that culminated with his election as President of Brazil in 2002. Above he is pictured greeting US President Barack Obama in 2010.

ABOVE In his eight years of office, President Lula visited more than 80 countries. His pragmatic and trade-oriented foreign policy meant that he circulated with ease among leaders as diverse as the late Venezuelan President Hugo Chávez (above), Iranian leader Mahmoud Ahmadinejad, and their American counterparts George W. Bush and Barack Obama.

LEFT The 21 years under the military regime are still fresh in the memory of many Brazilians, especially those whose relatives were arrested, tortured or killed. In 2012, hundreds of human rights activists and members of left-wing parties protested against a meeting organised by Rio's Military Club to mark the 48th anniversary of the coup.

ABOVE The first woman to become president of Brazil, Dilma Rousseff (1947–) joined guerilla groups during the military regime, when she was imprisoned and allegedly tortured between 1970 and 1972. After serving as President Lula's minister of energy, then his chief-of-staff, he backed her as his successor in the electoral campaign of 2010.

TOP Protesters wave banners and posters with pictures of tortured and disappeared people at the demonstration outside the Military Club in Rio. In 2011, the Brazilian Congress approved the creation of the National Truth Commission to investigate human rights violations during the period between 1946 and 1988, which includes the military regime. The organization, however, has received strong criticism from both human rights activists and the military.

PEOPLE – A NATION OF DIVERSITY

Home to age-old indigenous tribes and hypermodern cities, Brazil is a nation of astounding diversity. The intermixing of African, European and indigenous bloodlines over the years has created a complex collage of colours and creeds. Add to this ethnic variety the millions of immigrants hailing from every corner of the globe who flooded into the country in the late nineteenth and early twentieth centuries. With roots stretching back to Africa, Europe, the Middle East and Asia, it's no easy task to define a "typical Brazilian".

THE INDIGENOUS

Brazil's indigenous culture has played a role in shaping the country's folklore, its dance, music and even the cuisine. Among key foods are tapioca, *manioc* (cassava/yuca), potatoes, cashew nuts, *mate* (a tea-like beverage made from the dried leaves of the yerba mate plant) and *guaraná* (a native Amazonian plant whose caffeine-filled fruit has long been used as a stimulant). European colonists quickly adopted the native custom of sleeping in hammocks, and noted their attentive hygiene – bathing several times a day in the river or sea – which left an indelible mark on fastidious Brazilian habits of today. *Carnaval* (see chapter 3) costumes, replete with feathers and body paint, evolved from indigenous garb mingled with African rhythms and European tradition.

The consumption of human flesh, as practised by a few tribes, also contributed to some notion of Brazilian identity. In the 1920s, the intellectual movement of anthropophagy (a fancy word for cannibalism) came to denote Brazil's lust for new ideas and culture that would be consumed, digested and subsequently transformed into something uniquely Brazilian. Thereafter, Brazilians would use this metaphoric cannibalism to help explain the nation's prodigious cultural output from music and film to theatre, the visual arts and architecture.

Located mostly in the Amazon, Brazil's indigenous population today numbers over 750,000 people, representing 200 different tribes – including an estimated 60 non-contacted peoples. Although this is a fraction of the 2,000-plus tribes existing prior to the European arrival, the indigenous population has shown a remarkable resurgence over the last 40 years. The population has tripled since 1970, which is all the more surprising considering the continued threats to the indigenous communities – including logging, mining, ranching, and the building of roads, settlements and hydroelectric dams.

THE AFRICANS

African roots run deep in Brazil. More than 50 per cent of the country's 200 million inhabitants claim some form of African ancestry, and only one country in the world (Nigeria) has more black people than Brazil. Afro-Brazilians have made an enormous contribution to the nation's culture, creating some of Brazil's best music, shaping its most famous celebrations and inventing its best-loved culinary dishes.

Some of Brazil's most acclaimed cuisine has African roots. *Feijoada*, a stew made of black beans and pork served over rice, originated in the slave quarters of colonial plantations, and has since become the national dish. The music of samba, with its African movements and rhythms, was created by Afro-Brazilians in the early nineteenth century and later became inextricably linked to the revelry of *carnaval*. Even the Portuguese spoken in Brazil, with its more melodic quality and unique expressions such as *bunda* (backside) and *cafuné* (the caressing of another's head), show the African influence on the language.

Slaves also brought with them their African religions, which evolved over the years into *Candomblé*. This polytheistic religion, with its elements of magic and mysticism, blended with the Roman Catholicism of the Portuguese and the animist beliefs of the Amerindians. Like gods in Greek mythology, the deities all have unique personalities and mythologies. To keep their religion alive, slaves also juxtaposed Catholic and African saints and religious symbols. Ogum, the god of iron and war, became the alter ego of dragon-slaying St George, while Yemanjá, the blue-robed goddess of the sea, was otherwise known as the Virgin Mary.

The practice of *Candomblé* is strongest in the Northeast, the Afro-Brazilian stronghold, and many of the festivals there have a *Candomblé* connection. In ceremonies, participants chant songs in Yoruba (a West African language), women wearing hooped skirts begin a slow circular dance, while drummers pound out rhythms of increasing tempo as the night wears on. A celebratory atmosphere prevails, with dancers falling into trances or whirling like dervishes as they feel the presence of their *orixá*, or deity. *Candomblé* followers believe that each person has a particular god watching over them, and the ceremony provides the opportunity to interact with that deity. While *Candomblé* remains predominantly a practice of Afro-Brazilians, some white Brazilians have also become members, including the novelist Jorge Amado, the artist Carybé and singer and political activist Caetano Veloso.

THE IMMIGRANTS

Over the centuries, wave upon wave of immigrants have also shaped modern-day Brazil. Most prominent are the Portuguese, who bequeathed the country its language, religion and festival calendar, its social class system and to a certain degree its ideology. Portugal's non-domineering approach to the running of its colony helped preserve Brazil's cohesion after its independence in 1822 (in contrast to the violent break-up of Spanish Latin America around the same time) and its distaste for violence led to relatively peaceful transitions when slavery was abolished, which in turn fed the perception that Brazilians were a nonviolent people. Even after Brazil became a republic in 1889, officially doing away with the monarchy, immigrants continued to arrive from Portugal. Between the 1880s and the 1950s some 1.5 million or 30 per cent of the total influx hailed from Portugal.

In the nineteenth and early twentieth centuries, more Italians immigrated into the country than any other group — more than a million arrived between 1890 and 1919. Some came to work on the coffee plantations after slavery was abolished, while a steady stream made their way to São Paulo, where their labour fuelled the growth of the burgeoning metropolis. As their numbers swelled, Italians led the nation's early efforts toward unionizing; other Italians became entrepreneurs, succeeding by dint of intelligence, hard work and helpful family connections. Some of Brazil's most prominent industrialists of the early twentieth century hailed from Italy. Francesco Matarazzo became the most successful of the Italian emigrés. Born in Salerno in the southwest of Italy, he moved to São Paulo at the age of 26, and went from a sales clerk to the head of a nationwide empire of wheat, cotton and textile mills, ships, railways, distilling and many other industries. When he died in 1937 at the age of 83, his vast empire made him the wealthiest man in Brazil.

Germans settled in the more temperate southern states, introducing their Protestant faith and founding some of Brazil's first breweries. Blumenau, in the southern state of Santa Catarina, is known for its alpine architecture, local schnitzel and bratwurst restaurants, and one of the largest Oktoberfests outside of Germany. Blue-eyed, blonde-haired Brazilians and tidy Germanic towns are among their legacies. Italians also settled in the South, planting vineyards and opening wineries, which continue to flourish today.

The first Japanese arrived in the early 1900s and initially toiled in low-paying jobs on farms and coffee plantations. As time passed, the community started up their own farms and collectives, and by the 1930s the Japanese were already contributing to some 35 per cent of fruit and vegetable production in the São Paulo region. Despite the oppressive discrimination they faced, the Japanese community flourished and today they are considered one of Brazil's most successful and well-integrated communities. Many Nisei and Sansei (second- and third-generation Japanese) hold high-ranking positions in government, finance, business and academia. They also remain quite active in the agricultural sector; large Japanese-run farm cooperatives continue to supply most of the fruit and vegetables for the Rio and São Paulo markets. An estimated 1.5 million Brazilians are of Japanese descent, and São Paulo is home to the largest Japanese population outside of Japan.

After the First World War, Brazil saw an even wider variety of immigrants, hailing from other parts of Europe. Polish, Russians and Romanians came, many of whom sought refuge from the political turmoil happening across the continent. During the rise of Nazism in Europe, Jews arrived in successive waves, as did Nazis looking to avoid trial for war crimes after the Second World War. In the 1970s, civil war in Lebanon brought tens of thousands of Lebanese to Brazil's shores, along with smaller numbers of Syrians and Palestinians. They added to the approximately 200,000 Middle Eastern and Arab immigrants who had settled in Brazil in the half-century prior.

REGIONAL DIFFERENCES

Ancestry Is only part of the equation when it comes to the Brazilian identity. Given the remarkable mixing and blending over the years, Brazilians are equally conscious of one's regional background — often accompanied by colourful, not always accurate stereotypes. In the Amazon, copper-skinned caboclos (of mixed Indigenous-European heritage) are known for keeping alive the traditions of their ancestors in folklore fests. Gaúchos, who populate Rio Grande do Sul, are stereotyped as being chaps-wearing, mate-drinking cowboys, while baianos (residents of Bahia) have a reputation for being extrovert and more interested in partying than work (indeed the Northeast has far more festivals and holidays than any other state). Sertanejos (residents of the drought-prone sertão, or backlands) are considered a tenacious group, with strong folk traditions. Mineiros (residents from the landlocked state of Minas Gerais) are seen as more reserved than coastal dwellers. Meanwhile, cariocas (residents of Rio de Janeiro) are stereotyped for being superficial and overly body conscious by paulistas (residents of São Paulo) — who in turn are derided for their fast-paced lifestyle and cold bearing. All of which leads to good-natured teasing (and exciting football matches) when the different states come together.

ABOVE Throughout the late nineteenth and early twentieth centuries, several expeditions crossed indigenous territory, mainly with economic goals. The missions underwent great changes after military officer Cândido Rondon founded the Indian Protection Service. Rondon accompanied US President Theodore Roosevelt on his legendary expedition to the Amazon in 1913–14.

OPPOSITE This 1880 illustration depicts the Mundurucú people, who live on the left bank of the Tapajós River. The image describes the tribe's excruciatingly painful puberty rite. Teenagers dance and sing after having had their hands placed in gloves made of palm tree bark filled with masses of biting ants.

RIGHT Brazil has an estimated indigenous population of over 890,000 people, according to the latest census. Over 57 per cent of those live in indigenous lands, which occupy 12.5 per cent of the entire Brazilian territory and to which they have exclusive possession.

RIGHT Some indigenous groups have managed to preserve their traditions, such as the Kuarup festival, here observed by girls from the Awara population in the Amazon region, in 2005. It comprises rituals to honour their ancestors and wrestling competitions.

BELOW RIGHT Members of several indigenous groups attend a public hearing of the Human Rights Commission at the National Congress in Brasília in December 2012. In recent years, Brazil's native inhabitants have faced severe challenges posed by logging, mining and ranching and have become more vocal in demanding their rights.

OPPOSITE One of several contentious issues regarding Brazil's indigenous populations nowadays is the Belo Monte dam project, near Altamira in the Amazon basin. The region that will host the world's third-largest hydroelectric project will see as much as 154 square miles (400 square kilometers) of its rainforest area flooded.

PREVIOUS PAGE Members of the Awati tribe arrive on bicycles in an area of the Amazon forest occupied by the Awara tribe, in central Brazil, to take part in the Kuarup ceremony. The Kuarup ceremony is held around a wooden structure, ritually built to represent the spirits of the deceased. Brazil's indigenous inhabitants today represent merely 0.4 per cent of the country's population (Le Monde). Although the current 305 groups are only a fraction of the 2,000-plus tribes to exist prior to the European arrival, the indigenous population has shown a remarkable resurgence over the last 40 years, tripling since 1970.

LEFT Indigenous people from several tribes gathered at the Rio+20 summit. In the document they produced at the event, they expressed their opposition to large-scale projects affecting indigenous territories, including the Belo Monte and Jirau hydroelectric dams, as well as highway, biofuel and mining projects.

ABOVE Introduced diseases, enslavement and armed conflict have decimated Brazil's indigenous population over the centuries. Although they still face regular attacks by loggers and prospectors, Brazil's indigenous peoples have shown great endurance. The country is believed to be home to up to 60 uncontacted tribes, which means it has the greatest number of isolated inhabitants in the world.

RIGHT An indigenous family attending the United Nations Conference on Sustainable Development in 2012 (the Rio+20 summit). By the end of the event, along with indigenous peoples from all over the world, they signed a declaration claiming violations of their inherent rights are on the increase.

ABOVE The only country in the world that has more people of African descent than Brazil is Nigeria. In spite of its great contribution to Brazilian culture, the country's vast Afro-Brazilian population has often found the path to social mobility difficult.

ABOVE A family in Rio de Janeiro in 1867. Although the slavery of indigenous people was officially ended in the eighteenth century, Africans and their descendants would not be freed until 1888. Steps towards abolition were taken gradually, first with the ban of slave trafficking, then with a law liberating all the children of slaves born after September 1871.

LEFT On the last days of each year, Brazilians in Rio and other coastal cities gather by the beach to honour Yemanjá, Goddess of the Sea and one of the main deities of the Afro-Brazilian religion of *Candomblé*. The ritual comprises dressing in white and offering flowers and gifts to the goddess.

TOP Almost 600,000 Brazilians define themselves as followers of any sort of Afro-Brazilian religion, the vast majority of them with Umbanda. This faith combines elements of many African religions, such as the worship of Orishas, with Catholicism and Spiritism.

ABOVE Yemanjá is also celebrated on February 2, when the faithful offer her gifts such as flowers, perfumes and jewellery. They dance in a circle and sing ancestral Yoruba prayers, sometimes entering a trance. Yemanjá is also worshipped in Cuba and Uruguay, but the strongest cult is in Bahia.

ABOVE After abolishing slavery in the nineteenth century, Brazil instigated an open-door policy to attract new immigrants, aiming to simultaneously replace the loss of labour and to whiten the country's ethnic mix. Among the millions heeding the call were immigrants from Italy, who worked in manufacturing, textiles, agriculture and retail, such as the family posing here for a photo in their shoe store, c.1930.

PREVIOUS PAGE A woman wearing traditional adornments takes part in the Bonfim festivities in Salvador, Bahia. The northern state of Bahia exemplifies Brazil's religious tolerance, with devotees of the Afro-Brazilian religion of *Candomblé* living peacefully alongside Catholics. During January's Festa do Bonfim, the most traditional syncretic celebration in Salvador, the faithful gather for a procession toward the Bonfim Church, where they wash its stairway.

ABOVE In the nineteenth and early twentieth centuries, a greater number of Italians immigrated to Brazil than any other group – more than one million arrived between 1890 and 1919. Some came to work on the coffee plantations of the countryside outside São Paulo, while a steady stream made their way to the state capital itself, where their labour fuelled the growth of the burgeoning metropolis.

LEFT Founded in 1850, Blumenau is known for its alpine architecture and local schnitzel and bratwurst restaurants. It hosts one of the largest Oktoberfests outside Germany. The 2011 event received over 560,000 visitors, who consumed more than 600,000 litres (131,981 gallons) of beer.

BELOW LEFT After Brazil entered the World War II on the Allied side in 1942, anti-German sentiment and riots took place in several cities with large immigrant communities. Factories, shops and hotels were destroyed by mobs and local police persecuted citizens from Germany, Italy and Japan. When the war was over, German schools like the one pictured here in Rio, in 1937, were not reopened.

OPPOSITE A German immigrant preparing traditional food, 1939. Germans settled in the more temperate Southern states, introducing their Protestant faith and founding some of Brazil's first breweries. Blue-eyed, blond-haired Brazilians and tidy Germanic-looking towns are among their legacies. They even influenced local gastronomy, with bratwurst sausages and potato salad becoming typical bar food in many Brazilian cities.

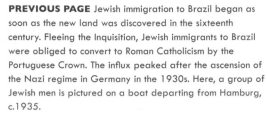

PREVIOUS PAGE Jewish immigration to Brazil began as soon as the new land was discovered in the sixteenth century. Fleeing the Inquisition, Jewish immigrants to Brazil were obliged to convert to Roman Catholicism by the Portuguese Crown. The influx peaked after the ascension of the Nazi regime in Germany in the 1930s. Here, a group of Jewish men is pictured on a boat departing from Hamburg, c.1935.

LEFT Many *nisei* and *sansei* (second- and third-generation Japanese) hold high-ranking positions in Brazilian government, finance, business and academia. They also remain quite active in the agricultural sector. They make up a local Japanese population around 1.5 million – the largest Japanese community outside Japan.

BELOW LEFT Adapting to a new life in Brazil proved to be a hard task for some of the early Japanese immigrants. Many dreamt of making enough money to be able to return home. Holding onto that hope, they taught the Japanese language and culture to their children in schools founded in the colonies where they lived.

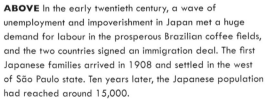

ABOVE In the early twentieth century, a wave of unemployment and impoverishment in Japan met a huge demand for labour in the prosperous Brazilian coffee fields, and the two countries signed an immigration deal. The first Japanese families arrived in 1908 and settled in the west of São Paulo state. Ten years later, the Japanese population had reached around 15,000.

ABOVE As time passed, the Japanese community started up their own farms and collectives, and by the 1930s, they were already contributing to some 35 per cent of the fruit and vegetable production in the São Paulo region.

PREVIOUS PAGE The town of Aparecida, in the state of São Paulo, attracts hundreds of thousands of pilgrims on October 12 each year. They gather at the National Sanctuary of Our Lady of Aparecida to celebrate the feast day of Brazil's patron saint. The crowd rivals only that of Círio de Nazaré, a procession in honour of Our Lady of Nazaré that takes place in Belém, attended by millions.

ABOVE With about 123 million self-declared Catholics, Brazil is the country with the largest Roman Catholic community in the world. Heavily influenced by Portuguese immigrants, who frequently brought missionaries with them, Brazil was only declared a secular state after the Republican Constitution of 1891.

TOP Millions of Pentecostal evangelicals gather on the streets of São Paulo every year for the March for Jesus. According to the 2010 census, some 25.3 million Brazilians declare themselves as followers of Pentecostal Evangelic churches – a 62 per cent increase in comparison to a decade earlier.

ABOVE Catholic nuns celebrate the holiday of Corpus Christi in Belém (2012). In recent years, the Roman Catholic Church in Brazil and the rest of Latin America has lost followers to other religions, mostly Protestantism.

ABOVE Families assemble for an informal portrait outside a row of single-storey houses in Natal, c.1931, when Brazil had a population of between 30 and 41 million. The intermixing of African, European and indigenous bloodlines over the years has created a complex collage of colours and creeds.

ABOVE Mixed race families have been common and widely accepted in Brazil ever since the first Portuguese settlers arrived. In its decennial census, Brazil uses the term *pardo* to include those of mixed ancestry. The group makes up 43 per cent of the population.

PREVIOUS PAGE A couple sits by the entrance to Rocinha, the largest *favela* (shanty town) in Rio. The southeastern region of Brazil, where the city is located, is the most ethnically diverse part of the country. The former capital was home to many Portuguese and African immigrants, a mix reflected today in its population.

LEFT People watch fireworks along Copacabana Beach, Rio during the first few minutes of January 1, 2013, at a party attended by up to three million each year. As part of the ritual for good fortune, those of different faiths (and even atheists) like to jump seven waves or simply "wash away the bad energy" with a dip in the sea.

ABOVE Every Easter, the city of Curitiba in southern Brazil hosts a festival of folkloric dance and music to celebrate the holiday. Here, a group of Brazilians of Polish descent perform the *Święconka*, a traditional dance meant to bless the Easter baskets.

ABOVE Dancers dressed in country costumes perform the
traditional folk dance, *quadrilha*, at the Calvário Church in
São Paulo. The traditional annual *Festa Junina* (June festival)
is celebrated nationwide with music, dances and food in
honour of the month's three Catholic saint days: Saint
Anthony, Saint John the Baptist and Saint Peter. A fictitious
shotgun-style wedding is often part of the merriment as
pictured here.

ABOVE In Brazil, members of different religions can coexist in harmony. During the Israel–Hezbollah War in Lebanon, in 2006, members of the Lebanese and Jewish communities in Rio de Janeiro got together to march in demand of a ceasefire and peace talks – not before indulging in a typical Lebanese meal.

ABOVE A group of Jewish-Brazilians take part in a rally organized by the Israeli community living in São Paulo, calling for peace in the Middle East (August 2006).

RIGHT Ancestry is only part of the equation when it comes to Brazilian identity. Given the remarkable mixing and blending over the years, Brazilians are equally conscious of regional background. Brazilians born in Rio, or *cariocas*, such as the girls pictured here, are labelled as fun and friendly.

RIGHT The recent economic boom has attracted a new wave of immigrants to Brazil, many of whom come from neighbouring countries. According to official sources, some 350,000 Bolivian immigrants, such as the family pictured here, are living in São Paulo – many of them illegally.

ABOVE In the Amazon region, Portuguese and Spanish colonizers encountered indigenous peoples when they first raided the area in the seventeenth century. The exploitation of rubber in the early twentieth century attracted workers from the impoverished northeast, adding a mixed race element to the melting pot of local ethnicities.

ABOVE Besides the ethnic mix, geographic factors were
crucial in forming the diversity of the Brazilian population.
In the cooler Southern state of Rio Grande do Sul, which
borders Argentina and Uruguay, the *gaúchos* (cowboys)
maintain to this day their habit of drinking *chimarrão,* a
bitter infused drink also known as *mate.*

ABOVE Nowadays, many descendants of Jewish immigrants make their way to Israel to learn more about their origins, but without forgetting Brazil. Here, a group of youngsters watch the 2006 World Cup match between Brazil and Croatia at Kibbutz Bror Chayil, founded in Israel by Brazilian Jews.

RIGHT Buddhist monks of Busshinji Temple attend an early-morning meditation session on a helipad atop the Copan building, in São Paulo. Once a month, they climb 37 floors for the ritual. The 2010 census estimates that Brazil has around 200,000 Buddhists, a religion brought to the country by the Japanese immigrants in the twentieth century.

THE CULTURAL BEAT OF BRAZIL

Influences from both the new and old worlds have shaped Brazil's dynamic culture, which extends across many fields, from music and fine arts to cinema, sports and fashion. The nation's wildly colourful festivals, lilting *bossa novas* and roaring football matches, are known across the globe, while the enormous, ever-evolving cultural output continues to be the nation's greatest source of pride.

THE WORLD'S BIGGEST STREET PARTY

Although *carnaval* is deeply associated with Rio, it's celebrated with abandon across the whole of Brazil. The pre-Lenten festival features all-night concerts, dancing in the streets and costumed balls, attracting merry-makers from around the world. Officially just five days of revelry (the Friday to Tuesday preceding Ash Wednesday), in reality the festivities begin weeks in advance.

Every city throws a party, which takes many different forms and features a multitude of unique rhythms. In the Northeastern city of Salvador, well-known bands play atop huge trucks packed with speakers, while revellers dance through the streets behind them. Further north, Olinda's historic centre becomes the backdrop to giant puppets, wildly costumed festival-goers and bands playing *frevo* (fast brass-band beats) and *maracatu* (a slow, heavy Afro-Brazilian rhythm). In Paraty, a few hours south of Rio, several thousand enthusiasts cover themselves in mud and shamble, caveman-style, along the beach.

Perhaps not surprisingly, Rio de Janeiro in Brazil's Southeast throws the biggest *carnaval* of all, with several hundred street parties across town, followed by the huge all-night parades in a custom-built arena called the *sambódromo*. Before a crowd of some 90,000, each of Rio's leading 12 samba schools compete for top honours, with a procession of giant mechanized floats, heart-pounding drum corps and thousands of elaborately costumed dancers. Every local has a favourite school, and the crowds join in, wearing the school colours and singing the theme song as they dance in the aisles.

SAMBA

The music of Rio's *carnaval* is samba, a richly varied style and a deeply ingrained part of city life. Samba comes in many forms, from the thundering *samba enredo* played by samba schools during *carnaval* parades to the more melodic, lyrically rich *samba-canção* and the big-band dancehall-style *samba de gafieira*. Samba first emerged in early twentieth-century Rio in a poor neighbourhood of migrants from the Northeast. Old Bahian matriarchs (referred to as *tias*, or aunts) opened up their homes to gatherings of music, dance and worship (revolving around the Afro-Brazilian religion of *Candomblé*. The creatively charged atmosphere gave rise to some of the world's first sambas, which coincided with early *carnaval* parades. Over the years, samba continued to evolve, going from a marginal music of the streets to the city's golden soundtrack.

BOSSA NOVA

The seductive melodies of *bossa nova* (which means approximately 'new trend') emerged in the 1950s, also in Rio, and sparked a new era of Brazilian music. Bossa nova's founding fathers were songwriter Antônio Carlos Jobim and lyricist-poet Vinícius de Moraes. The two slowed down the basic samba rhythm and incorporated elements of jazz and classical music to create an intimate, more harmonic sound. Guitarist João Gilberto helped popularize the music with his melodic understated singing and syncopated playing. Marcel Camus' film *Orfeu Negro* (Black Orpheus), released in 1959, introduced bossa nova to the world by means of an extraordinary soundtrack by Jobim, de Moraes and guitarist-composer Luiz Bonfá. The theme song "Manhã de Carnaval" (Morning of Carnival) by Bonfá became a worldwide hit, as did later bossa nova songs such as Jobim's "Corcovado" (named after the famous mountain in Rio, atop which looms the statue of Christ the Redeemer) and the Jobim and de Moraes' much-loved "Garota de Ipanema" (The Girl from Ipanema).

TROPICÁLIA

Other pivotal styles of music emerged in the decades that followed. In the late 1960s, *tropicália* (a word that pays homage to Brazil's tropical setting) hit the airwaves. Bahian singers Caetano Veloso and Gilberto Gil led the movement, fusing elements of psychedelic rock, blues, samba and bossa nova to create a brash, cinematic sound. Tropicália was not only a musical movement, but also embraced in theatre, poetry, painting and sculpture. One of the most famous artworks from the time is Hélio Oiticica's installation entitled "Tropicália" — an elaborate environment of sand, water, banana trees, parrots and a television set that invited viewers into the scene. Songs from this period took aim at the military dictatorship, and the movement largely died out when Veloso and Gil were sent into exile in 1969. The two were arrested in December 1968 during the dictatorial presidency of General Costa e Silva. After spending several months in prison, the pair were released on condition they leave the country, which they did, living in London for the next three years. Although *tropicália* was finished by 1970, the movement had a significant influence on the era of musical experimentation that would follow.

MPB & BEYOND

MPB, or *Música Popular Brasileiro* (popular Brazilian music) also emerged in the late 1960s and early 1970s. The all-encompassing catchphrase defines music that doesn't fit into a neat category. Artists from this period incorporated different elements in their music from protest lyrics to funk, folk and rock 'n' roll. Jorge Ben Jor, Elis Regina, Djavan and Chico Buarque are among the many great artists who launched careers during this time.

In the last few decades, Brazilian music has continued to evolve, creating new sounds, from lush, electro grooves to the hard-hitting hip-hop from the *favelas*. Regional styles also proliferate: the lively partner-dancing beats of *forró* are popular across the country, while the sensual rhythms of *carimbó* are at present little known outside of the Amazon.

THE BEAUTIFUL GAME

Brazil may be the most Catholic country on earth (with over 120 million self-declared members), but the nation's true religion is football. No one goes to work on big international game days, with everyone packing into neighbourhood bars or on the sidewalks out front to watch the game. After a big win, every city in the country erupts with rowdy nights of partying.

Brazilians play some of the world's most creative and thrilling football. They are the only country to win the World Cup five times and to compete in every tournament. Brazil has raised many legendary players through its ranks, from the Afro-Brazilian Leônidas da Silva — who helped break down racial barriers and scored the only bicycle kick goal (an acrobatic kick in which a player kicks the ball over his head) ever in World Cup history in 1938 — to Romario, a powerful striker who scored over 900 goals during his career. The greatest of all though must be Pelé, sometimes simply referred to as "O Rei" (the king). Throughout his 22-year career, the teams he played on secured 53 titles, including three World Cups (the first, in Sweden in 1958, when he was just 17 years old). By the time Pelé retired in 1977, he had played in 1,366 games and scored over 1,200 goals, making him one of the world's greatest all-time goal scorers.

CAPOEIRA & OTHER SPORTS

Brazil is more than a one-hit wonder when it comes to sport, having produced some of the world's top volleyball players, surfers, martial artists, rodeo riders and Formula One drivers (including the legendary Ayrton Senna, still considered one of the finest drivers in the history of motorsport). More uniquely home-grown is capoeira, a martial art developed by Afro-Brazilian slaves as a form of self defence against their captors. Referred to as a jogo (game), which one "plays", capoeira combines elements of fighting and dancing, emphasizing strength, acrobatics and self-control; generally there is no contact. A long, one-stringed percussion instrument called the berimbau dictates the tempo of the fight, while spectators clap and sing along. Popular in the Northeast, where it originated, capoeira is practised throughout Brazil and in many other countries across the globe. According to legend capoeira was created by African slaves some time in the 17th or 18th centuries, although its first official recording doesn't appear until 1818 in a police report in Rio de Janeiro.

CINEMA

Brazil has a flourishing film industry, though few of its productions make it onto the world's screens. Its novelas (soap operas), on the other hand, are a much-loved export to over 100 countries. Unlike American soap operas, novelas often have racier subject matter and are set in historical periods — on a nineteenth-century coffee plantation, for instance — and run for less than a year, with characters killed off along the way! With tens of millions of viewers tuning in nightly in Brazil, novelas have become an entrenched part of society. The series often feature high-profile actors — such as the Oscar-nominated actress Fernando Montenegro who starred in the novela Belíssima (Beautiful) in 2006. The shows also net huge sums of advertising revenue. Avenida Brasil, which aired in 2012, earned about R$1 billion (£329 million) over its seven-month run.

The film industry has been going strong since the 1960s, when Brazil was known for its cinema novo (new cinema) movement. Influenced by Italian Neorealism and French New Wave, films made in this time focused on the country's bleak social problems and class struggle. Glauber Rocha was one of cinema novo's most important filmmakers. He made critically acclaimed films such as Black God, White Devil (1964), which depicts a violent land of mysticism and realism in the drought-stricken sertão (backlands).

One of the top directors of recent years is Walter Salles, whose road movie-cum-buddy film Central Station (1998) won an Academy Award in 1999. Salles's other hits include The Motorcycle Diaries (2004), charting Che Guevara's epic South American journey, and On the Road (2012), a cinematic version of the Kerouac classic. Brazil's other top director is Fernando Meirelles, who directed City of God (2002), which depicts the brutality and redemption in a Rio favela. The film received four Academy Award nominations in 2004, and it was named by Time magazine as one of the top 100 films of all time. Meirelles went on to direct The Constant Gardener (2002) and Blindness (2008).

ARTFUL BACKDROPS

Brazil's striking landscapes — from the futuristic cityscapes of São Paulo to the beautiful beaches of Rio — have played no small role in the nation's art, pop culture and fashion scenes. Photographer Sebastião Salgado does an exquisite job of capturing the rawness and beauty of the country's landscapes, while street artists Os Gêmeos (the twins) transform urban spaces into evocatively playful canvasses. The twin brothers are among a new crop of talented Brazilians making names for themselves in the global art scene. As part of the cultural events held in conjunction with the recent Summer Olympics, thirty Brazilian artists were invited to take part in the London 2012 Festival. The artists showcased their work in some of London's most revered exhibition halls, including the Tate Modern and the Victoria and Albert Museum.

Meanwhile, top Brazilian fashion designers, such as Alexandre Herchcovitch and Carlos Miele, continue to create eye-catching designs ideal for the streets of Ipanema and beyond. Also in the fashion industry, Brazilian supermodel Gisele Bündchen continues to turn heads — and not merely for her bikini-clad photo shoots. The model and occasional actress — she played supporting roles in the films Taxi (2004) and The Devil Wears Prada (2006) — was named in 2009 a goodwill ambassador for the United Nations Environment Programme (UNEP) in order to raise awareness for environmental threats like global warming and deforestation.

LEFT Grande Rio samba school parading through the *sambódromo* during Rio's *carnaval*. Although *cariocas* (native inhabitants of Rio de Janeiro) have been celebrating *carnaval* since the eighteenth century, it was in the 1920s that the popularity of samba prompted the creation of societies, or schools, in deprived communities around Rio. Today, celebrities, unknown members of the public and foreign tourists are equally welcome to take part in the show.

ABOVE *Carnaval* revellers in Salvador, capital of the northeastern state of Bahia.

LEFT Every Brazilian city throws a different party during *carnaval*. In the northeast, Olinda's historic centre becomes the backdrop to giant puppets, wildly costumed festival-goers and bands playing *frevo* (fast brass-band beats) and *maracatu* (a slow, heavy Afro-Brazilian rhythm).

LEFT AND RIGHT Dancers at Rio de Janeiro *carnaval*. The painstakingly handmade garments worn by dancers in the parade represent the themes of the different samba schools and draw inspiration from the vast mix of cultures to be found across Brazil.

RIGHT Broadcast to millions across Brazil and elsewhere, the samba school parade in Rio is a high-profile event among Brazilian celebrities. One of the most coveted roles in the two-day show is the *rainha da bateria* (drum queen), given by each school to prominent actresses, models and TV presenters. Here, former *Big Brother Brasil 3* (2003) contestant Sabrina Sato performs for Unidos de Vila Isabel samba school.

ABOVE The main parade in Rio is a fierce competition between the city's most traditional samba schools. Each school puts on a show according to a theme and must follow strict rules for the sequence and timing of the parade. Every *carioca* has a favourite school, such as União da Ilha do Governador, spectators show their passionate support when scores given by judges are announced on Ash Wednesday.

OPPOSITE Although *carnaval* is celebrated all across Brazil, it is in Rio where the party acquires an international dimension. The highlight is the all-night parade in a custom-built arena, the *sambódromo*. Before a crowd of 90,000, Rio's top samba schools – such as the Mangueira, pictured here – compete for top honours, with a procession of thousands of costumed dancers.

ABOVE A samba school sculptor works on a float in a workshop in Rio de Janeiro. *Carnaval* preparations begin months before the parade at the *sambódromo*. Samba schools hire professional artists who, according to a selected theme, create allegorical floats, costumes, sculptures and music for the final show. Unknown members of the samba schools carry out most of the everyday work.

OPPOSITE Apart from the samba school parade in the *sambódromo*, dozens of *blocos* (organized street bands and groups) take to the streets of Rio's neighbourhoods, promoting a free and more spontaneous party. Here, a reveller performs during the Banda de Ipanema parade, which, since 1965, has attracted thousands of people to Ipanema Beach.

LEFT Brazilian singer and musician João Gilberto strums his guitar in front of a microphone during a studio session in the 1980s. Considered to be one of the co-creators of bossa nova, Gilberto helped popularize the music with his melodic, understated singing and syncopated playing.

ABOVE Bahian singer Gilberto Gil, alongside his fellow countryman Caetano Veloso, led the movement known as *Tropicália* in the late 1960s, fusing elements of psychedelic rock, blues, samba and bossa nova to create a brash, cinematic sound. *Tropicália* was also embraced in theatre, poetry and the plastic arts.

ABOVE A *Candomblé* worshipper becomes possessed during the festival of Yemanjá, the goddess of the sea, in Salvador, Bahia. Yemanjá, originally from the ancient Yoruba mythology, is one of the most popular *orixás*, the deities from the Afro-Brazilian religion of *Candomblé*. Worshippers, usually dressed in traditional white, gather on the beach at dawn to leave offerings for their goddess, – including flowers, perfume and jewellery – and for music and dancing.

RIGHT A woman playing the guitar on a street in Salvador, Bahia, in celebration of *Dia do Samba,* which commemorates the day legendary samba composer Ary Barroso first visited Salvador on December 2, 1938.

LEFT Samba musicians play at the open-air Pedra do Sal, Rio de Janeiro. Originating in Bahia, the rhythm is recognized as a symbol of Brazil. It comes in many forms, from the thundering *samba-enredo* played by samba schools during *carnaval* parades to the more melodic, lyrically rich *samba-canção* and the big band dancehall style *samba de gafieira*.

TOP Born in the poor neighbourhood of Candeal, in Salvador, Carlinhos Brown is one of Brazil's most celebrated artists. A percussionist and composer, his music mixes influences of African rhythms, samba and reggae. He is also dedicated to social projects that involve teaching music and other arts to children from disadvantaged backgrounds in his hometown.

ABOVE One of the leaders of the *Tropicália* movement, Caetano Veloso became an internationally acclaimed artist, pictured in concert, 2010. His music in the 1960s took aim at the military dictatorship, and the *Tropicália* movement largely died out when Veloso and Gilberto Gil were exiled to London in 1969.

PREVIOUS An estimated million people attend a free concert by Gilberto Gil and Stevie Wonder at Copacabana Beach on December 25, 2012. The famous beauty spot is no stranger to large crowds, hosting Rio's official New Year fireworks display, which attracts more than two million revellers each year.

ABOVE A *baile funk* party in the Rocinha neighbourhood of Rio de Janeiro. *Funk carioca*, which is played at the parties, is a type of dance music that originated in Rio in the 1980s.

ABOVE *Funk carioca* artist Alex Cutler, more commonly known by his stage name Don Blanquito, performing at a club in the Irajá neighborhood of Rio de Janeiro.

LEFT The Companhia de Dança Deborah Colker won the
global stage with its blend of notable physical feats and
stunning visual imagery, in acts such as *Tatyana*, *Rota* and *Mix*
(pictured here during a rehearsal in Washington, DC). Rio-
born Colker is the mastermind behind the troupe and was
also the first woman to direct a Cirque du Soleil
performance, in 2009.

TOP One of the world's best-known photographers, Sebastião Salgado's work is marked by a profound social concern. Having studied to be an economist, the Minas Gerais-born artist took to photography during a 1973 mission to Africa. He has now travelled to over 100 countries for his photographic projects.

ABOVE Brazil's soap operas, known as *novelas*, are part of Brazilian daily life, being broadcast on prime time television and influencing behaviour, fashion and language across the country. Globo TV, who invest heavily in technology and quality, produce the most-watched series. Here, the crew follows a shooting of *Cordel Encantado* at Château de Chambord, in Chambord, Loir-et-Cher, France, in 2011.

ABOVE Fernando Meirelles' *City of God* (2002) put Brazil
firmly back on the global cinematic map. A brutal account of
life in a Rio *favela* (shanty town), it won numerous
international awards. Due to its success, Meirelles
has become one of the world's most respected filmmakers.

ABOVE Once known in Brazil as "poor man's sandals", Havaianas flip flops have turned the country's laidback beach style into a global trend. Annually, 162 million pairs are produced and sold to over 80 countries. It is estimated that two out of three Brazilians will wear a pair each year.

ABOVE Brazil's *enfant terrible* of fashion, Alexandre Herchcovitch, has gained a worldwide following with his daring collections, inspired by a fondness for clubbing and nightlife. His designs are seen on the catwalks of São Paulo, New York and Tokyo. Today, his portfolio also comprises footwear, computer apps and a range of striking jewellery.

ABOVE Street art in *Cidade de Deus* (City of God), part of the borough of Jacarepaguá, in the West Zone of Rio de Janeiro. The slum was immortalised in Fernando Meirelles' film of the same name in 2002.

TOP In the last decades, street art has become one of the distinguishing features of São Paulo's urban landscape. Initially frowned upon by local authorities, it is now hailed as a trademark of the city. Indeed some of its exponents, such as the duo Os Gêmeos (whose work is pictured here), have become renowned artists on the international circuit.

LEFT A group of men play dominoes next to a mural by street artist Speto in the Vila Magdalena neighbourhood of São Paulo.

TOP Brazilian art is some of the most cherished in the global market. Exponents of the *Tropicália* style, such as Hélio Oiticica and Lygia Pape (whose 1967 work *Roda dos Prazeres* – Wheel of Delights – is pictured here), became popular with respected museums in the 1960s and paved the way for artists working more recently, such as Adriana Varejão and Ernesto Neto.

ABOVE Cândido Portinari's mural diptypch, *War and Peace*, shown here during a 2010 exhibition in Rio, normally adorns the walls of the United Nations Building in New York City. Portinari was Brazil's first visual artist to gain international recognition, with museums such as New York's MoMA displaying his works. Exhibitions of his paintings have taken place all over the US and Europe.

OPPOSITE Born on a coffee plantation close to São Paulo, Cândido Portinari (1903–62), seen here painting in his studio in 1941, is one of the founding fathers of modern visual arts in Brazil. He broke with the classical European style, popular until then, by depicting peasants and poor workers, as well as the nation's exuberant character.

LEFT *Grand Nucleus* installation by Hélio Oiticica (1937–1980). One of the most groundbreaking Brazilian visual artists of the twentieth century, Oiticica was one of the key proponents of the *Tropicália* style. A vast amount of the artist's work was destroyed in a fire in 2009.

ABOVE Brazil's most popular modern writer, Jorge Amado (1912–2001), has seduced readers worldwide with his novels depicting the religious syncretism, profound social inequalities and sensuality of his home state of Bahia. Amado's works have been translated into 49 languages and also turned into highly successful TV series and feature films, such as *Dona Flor and Her Two Husbands* (1976), *Tieta* (1989) and *Gabriela* (1983).

LEFT Paulo Coelho's mystical and magical accounts have turned him into Brazil's most successful writer of all time. With titles such as *The Alchemist* (1988) and *Veronika Decides To Die* (1998), he has sold 100 million copies worldwide, and his novels have been translated into 66 different languages.

A football legend before the world's gaze. Pelé's last match for Santos, in October 1974, was a tearful moment for football fans. He had joined the team in 1956 at the age of 15. In 1975, he would sign with the New York Cosmos.

LEFT Romário de Souza Faria (known simply as Romário was unbeatable inside the box and managed to repeat Pelé's feat, striking more than 1,000 goals. He was also decisive in helping Brazil to win the 1994 World Cup, ending a 24-year period with no titles. The now-retired striker is as talented as he is sharp-tongued, a quality he currently displays as a politician.

ABOVE To Brazilians and football fans the world over, Edison Arantes do Nascimento (better known as Pelé) is not simply the finest player of all time, he is also hailed as O *Rei (The King)*, due to his many royal sporting attributes. Throughout his career, he scored over 1,200 goals and was the only player to have been three times champion of the world with a national squad.

RIGHT Up until this day, the 1970 Brazilian National Squad is hailed as one of the best teams to ever walk onto the pitch. Athletes such as Pelé, Jairzinho, Carlos Alberto Torres and Tostão played as a well rehearsed orchestra, applying the principles laid out by writer Nelson Rodrigues to whom "the blindest player is the one who sees nothing but the ball".

ABOVE Such is the passion surrounding the sport, the football glossary is known to many in Brazil, even those few not fully familiar with it. Here, for instance, Pelé performs one of his trademark moves: the overhead kick, known in Brazil as *bicicleta* (bicycle).

ABOVE The beautiful game is more than the nation's favourite sport. People from all walks of life play football across the whole of Brazil. The national squad is the only one to have secured five World Cup titles, and in 2014, aims to achieve a sixth at home.

TOP With 15 goals, The Phenomenon is the best striker in World Cup history. Ronaldo's story reads like the plot of a Brazilian soap opera. The working-class boy, who first became an international idol and then a wealthy businessman, or the comeback kid, who won a world title after many deemed him finished.

ABOVE Playing for Pelé's team, Santos, and many in Brazil trust that Neymar da Silva Santos (Neymar) hailed by many in Brazil as Pelé's natural successor as one of the future legends of the beautiful game. The 2014 World Cup will be an opportunity for the young striker to prove that he is more than just a joy to watch.

LEFT Whether on Ipanema Beach (pictured here) or in the massive asphalt jungle of São Paulo, Brazilians always find a time and a place to practise football. Many begin playing at a young age and those from more deprived backgrounds need to improvise for their practise, even making footballs out of socks.

ABOVE AND RIGHT São Paulo-born Ayrton Senna (1960–94) is widely regarded as one of the best Formula One World Championship drivers of all time, as well as one of the most daring. Audacious overtaking brought him admiration but also fierce rivalry from among his peers. His untimely death aged 34 on May 1 after his car crashed into a concrete barrier while leading the San Marino Grand Prix of 1994 at the Autodromo Enzo e Dino Ferrari in Italy is one of saddest stories of Brazilian sport. His death was regarded as a national tragedy and the Brazilian government declared three days of national mourning.

ABOVE In the last decade, Brazilian surfers have improved their skills to such an extent that many claim they are about to threaten the hegemony of US and Australia and conquer the world. A coastline as beautiful as Brazil's easily brings joy and exhilaration to this strenuous sport.

LEFT When it comes to sport, Brazil is more than a one-hit wonder, having produced some of the world's top surfers, martial artists, gymnasts, swimmers and volleyball players. Widely practised along the country's sandy beaches, beach volleyball has granted the nation a chain of medals since it first became an Olympic sport in 1996. In London 2012, the duo Juliana Silva (pictured) and Larissa França walked away with the bronze.

OPPOSITE In terms of medals in competitions, Brazilian swimmers still lag behind the world's powerhouses, but the country is improving steadily, with many of its athletes training abroad. Hopes for gold, boosted by César Cielo's performance in Beijing 2008, were not fulfilled in the 2012 London Olympic Games, but the team trust the home crowd will be a game changer in Rio 2016.

ABOVE Developed by African slaves in Brazil at the beginning of the sixteenth century, *capoeira* is a martial art that combines elements of dance and music. Having been regarded as a criminal activity and banned following the end of slavery in 1888, the art is now regarded as an intangible cultural heritage.

ABOVE The annual Barretos cowboy festival started out as a local attraction in 1956 and became Brazil's biggest rodeo. It epitomizes the culture of the increasingly rich Brazilian countryside and has become a global event that attracts international country music idols and Brazilian stars alike, such as Garth Brooks and Michel Teló.

THE WORLD'S NATURAL PARADISE

Vast in scale, Brazil is South America's giant, home to a staggering collection of wildlife-filled woodlands, tropical islands, thundering waterfalls, red-rock canyons and untamed rivers. Its verdant rainforests, teeming wetlands and diverse coastal environments have made the country a biodiversity hotspot, home to one of the largest collections of plant and animal life on the planet. Given its many natural wonders and great size – as the world's fifth largest country, Brazil borders every other nation on the continent except for Ecuador and Chile – perhaps it's no wonder Brazilians say "Deus é brasileiro" (God is Brazilian).

THE AMAZON

Covering almost half of Brazil, the Amazon occupies a near-mythic status among the world's rainforests. Its attributes boggle the imagination. Just 0.39 square miles (one square kilometre) of Amazonian rainforest can contain over 90,000 tonnes (180 million pounds) of living plants, including some 1,000 tree species. Amazonia's great biomass is often described as "the lungs of the world". In fact this patch of greenery – 2.7 million square miles (seven million square kilometres), of which four million are found in Brazil – produces 20 per cent of the world's oxygen and holds 20 per cent of its freshwater. This is the world's richest ecosystem, home to more than 55,000 plant species and more mammals, fish and amphibians than any other place on earth. Great cats, such as the jaguar, roam the forest floor, while howler monkeys, tamarins (squirrel-sized New World monkeys), marmosets and 80 other species of primate flourish among the jungle canopy. At times the Amazonian menagerie can seem like wildlife on steroids, from massive hog-sized capybara (the

world's largest rodent) to 10 m- (33 ft-) long caiman, giant anteaters and horse-sized Brazilian tapir – which can weigh up to 300 kg (661 lb).

One-fifth of the world's bird species lives in the Amazon. Its more colourful species include macaws, often spotted in pairs since these monogamous creatures mate for life. Powerful harpy eagles, broad-beaked toucans and iridescent hummingbirds, known in Portuguese as beija-flor (flower-kisser), are other iconic species.

The Amazon River itself flows east across the continent, generally along the equator, from the Andes to the Atlantic Ocean. It has numerous tributaries, about a dozen of which are larger than any river in Europe. Its immense volume exceeds the combined flow of the next eight largest rivers, and by the time it reaches the Atlantic, the main channel of the Amazon is enormous – about five times deeper than the Mississippi and also five times wider. The Amazon was once thought to be slightly shorter than the Nile, however a Brazilian expedition of 2007 pinpointed a new source high up in the Andes, some 6,800 km (4,225 miles) from the ocean, which would make it the world's longest river compared to the Nile's 6,695 km (4,160 miles) in length.

Amazonia's biodiversity doesn't end at the shoreline, though. Its rivers harbour more than 3,000 species of fish, including more than 100 catfish species. Among its largest fish species is the voracious pirarucu (one of world's largest freshwater fish), which can easily surpass 100 kg (220 lb) and grow to 2.4 m (7.8 ft) in length. The much mythologized piranha are scavengers, subsisting mostly on other fish, insects, plants and tree nuts and are not nearly so bloodthirsty as early explorers, such as Colonel

Percy Fawcett or Theodore Roosevelt, described – they pose a threat only to bleeding or wounded animals, and human fatalities are extremely rare. There are also giant river otters, slow-moving Amazon manatee (herbivorous marine mammals sometimes known as sea cows) and several varieties of freshwater dolphin. The boto, or pink dolphin, is the most famous, and is believed by some river dwellers to be a magical being. These dolphins have very poor eyesight but navigate and hunt by means of a highly complex sonar system.

THE PANTANAL

Although the Amazon tends to hog the spotlight, Brazil's other ecosystems are no less spectacular. In fact, the Pantanal, with its open spaces, offers even better opportunities for wildlife watching than the dense foliage of Amazonia. Although pantano means "swamp" in Portuguese and Spanish, the Pantanal is not a swamp but rather a vast (81,000 square miles/210,000 sq km) alluvial plain, comprising grassy savannah, forests and meadows. Lying near the geographic centre of South America, these wetlands were once part of an ancient inland sea, which began to dry up – along with the Amazon Sea – some 65 million years ago. During the rainy season (from November to March), rivers flood their banks, with water levels rising as much as 3 m (9.8 ft), inundating the low-lying grasses and sedges and creating small islands, where animals cluster. Owing to the hardships of cultivating the land amid such pronounced seasonal fluctuations, the human population here is low.

The diversity of wildlife in the Pantanal is spectacular, particularly after the seasonal floods arrive, submerging some 80 per cent of the landscape. Riverbanks are lined with countless caiman, well nourished by the piranha, catfish and other fish species. Giant otters frolic along the riversides, while marsh deer, tapir, fox and large families of capybara pad through the dense Pantanal grasses. Ibis, herons and egrets wade along the shoreline, while black-collared hawks and enormous hyacinth macaws soar overhead. Many species found in the Amazon are also found in the Pantanal, including jaguars, pumas, capuchin and howler monkeys and numerous other species – over 80 recorded species of mammal, and 650 bird species, according to UNESCO.

ATLANTIC RAINFOREST

Made up of dense, forest-covered mountains, wetlands and tropical islands, the Atlantic Rainforest contains one of the planet's highest concentrations of biodiversity. Some areas boast more than 450 different tree species in a single hectare, a variety unmatched anywhere else in the world. Named a UNESCO World Heritage site in 1999, the Atlantic Rainforest contains many unique species found nowhere else. This rich and complex ecosystem results from its partial isolation during the Ice Age. Here, the scenery is as spectacular as the wildlife, with green mountains running right down to the sea, along with waterfalls, wild rivers, beaches, lagoon systems and ocean-fronting sand dunes.

Sadly, centuries of human habitation and development have devastated the once luxuriant forest that stretched for more than 4,000 km (2,485 miles) along the coast of Brazil. Today only 7 per cent of the original forest is left, and it remains one of the world's most endangered habitats. Creatures under threat include woolly spider monkeys and the black-faced lion tamarin – one of South America's rarest primates, and only discovered in 1990.

ISLANDS

Brazil has no shortage of picturesque white sand beaches backed by swaying palms and fronting aquamarine seas. The coastline, which stretches some 7,500 km (4,660 miles), is dotted with idyllic islands that do a convincing imitation of paradise lost. One of the country's finest coastal settings is the ecotourism jewel of Fernando de Noronha, located 350 km (217 miles) off the coast of Natal. Twenty-one islands make up this picturesque archipelago, which is renowned worldwide for its coral reefs teeming with marine life. The crystal-clear waters make for some of Brazil's best diving, and its magnificent beaches are always free of crowds (limited flights keep visitor numbers under 350 per day). Large pods of spinner dolphins, hawksbill sea turtles and 230 species of fish are among the star attractions.

Other famous islands lie within a day's travel from major cities. Outside of Salvador, Morro de São Paulo has beaches, reefs, mangroves and even a few seventeenth-century ruins. Ilha Grande, near Rio de Janeiro, is a mountainous island with virgin tracts of Atlantic Rainforest. Visitors hike the forest paths to waterfalls and scenic beaches (of which there are more than 100), with the sounds of howler monkeys echoing through the treetops. On the São Paulo coast, Ilhabela (which means "beautiful island") lives up to its name with sheltered beaches, volcanic peaks and rainforest paths. Profuse wildlife inhabits the forested interior, including monkeys, toucans and other birdlife.

CHAPADA

The interior of Brazil conjures up the magic of outback travel, with big skies, jagged canyons and sandstone hills rolling across the plains. Scattered across several of the country's hinterland states are chapada, geologic formations of steeply carved sandstone cliffs ranging in elevation from 800 to 2,000 m (2,625 to 6,562 ft) above sea level. Waterfalls, natural swimming pools and magnificent flora create an oasis-like ambience amid the dry surrounding country of these spectacularly set chapada. The Chapada dos Veadeiros in Goiás state has the unusual *Vale da Lua* (valley of the moon), which invokes a lunar escape. The Chapada dos Guimarães in Mato Grosso is the unofficial geographic centre of South America, and its naturally formed *Cidade de Pedra* (stone city) resembles a stone temple jutting above the green valley floor far below. No less impressive is Bahia's Chapada Diamantina, a vast region of valleys and plateaux, waterfalls and crisp mountain streams amid the Sincorá Range.

IGUAÇU FALLS

Spread between Brazil and Argentina, these thundering waterfalls have long enchanted visitors. Hundreds of years before Europeans first laid eyes on them, Tupi-Guarani tribes used the falls as a sacred burial ground – in Guarani, the name Iguaçu (spelt "Iguazu" in Spanish) means great waters. And great they are: some 275 individual cascades, 80 m (262 ft) high and 3 km (9,842 ft) wide create one of the world's most awe-inspiring waterfalls. Subtropical rainforest surrounds the falls and is home to a wide variety of plant and animal life, including 2000 species of vascular plants, plus tapirs, giant anteaters, howler monkeys, toucans, macaws and harpy eagles.

OPPOSITE Crossed by the equator and sitting in low latitudes, the Amazon has a warm and wet climate. Temperatures do not vary much throughout the year, with an average of 23°C (73.4°F). The rainy season runs from November until June.

RIGHT Around 80 species of primate are believed to flourish among the jungle canopy. The brown capuchin monkey (*Sapajus apella*) can be found in the north and west areas of the Brazilian Amazon, as well as in Venezuela, Colombia, Ecuador, Peru and the Guyanas.

BOTTOM RIGHT The Amazon is home to more than 55,000 plant species, including the native *Victoria amazonica*. Its leaves can reach a diameter up to 2.5 m (8.2 ft) and can hold up to 40 kg (88 lb). Flowers blossom into a shade of white during the night, turning pink on the following day.

ABOVE The Amazon River flows east across South America. It has numerous tributaries, about a dozen of which are larger than any river in Europe. By the time it reaches the Atlantic Ocean, the main channel of the Amazon is about five times wider than the Mississippi River.

ABOVE View of Anavilhanas National Park, by the Rio Negro, in the state of Amazonas. Formed of hundreds of islands in an elongated shape covered by rainforest and creating an intricate net of channels, it is considered one of the most beautiful river landscapes in the world. In this section, the river is about 20 km (12.4 miles) wide.

ABOVE The rivers in the Amazon Basin harbour more than 3,000 species of fish and dozens of species of mammal. The Amazonian manatee (*Trichechus inunguis*) is the largest herbivorous creature in South American fresh waters. Its three-year reproductive cycle makes the introduction of new specimens more difficult and it is considered vulnerable by environmental authorities.

ABOVE An extremely rare picture of the Amazon boto or pink dolphin (*Inia geoffrensis*) in the Negro River, by the photographer and broadcaster Mark Cawardine. This potentially endangered aquatic mammal lives in such remote parts of the Amazon Basin that scientists cannot be sure how many survive.

RIGHT The Mamirauá Sustainable Development Reserve, an area of 57,000 sq km (22,000 sq miles) in the state of Amazonas, comprises flooded forest and wetland. It is home to around 6,000 people, mostly indigenous groups, who are allowed to exploit the region's natural resources in a sustainable manner.

ABOVE Two species of three-toed sloth live in the Amazon and are not considered endangered. Today, there are 311 species of mammal known to scientists in the ecosystem. Experts believe that more than 70 per cent of all the Amazonian animals have yet to receive a scientific name.

LEFT View of the Jamanxim River, in the state of Pará. Covering almost half of Brazil and often described as "the lungs of the world", the Amazon rainforest actually produces 20 per cent of the world's oxygen and holds 20 per cent of its freshwater.

ABOVE One-fifth of the world's bird species lives in
the Amazon. Green parrots (pictured) and macaws are
often spotted in pairs since these monogamous creatures
mate for life.

ABOVE Brazil's coastline stretches some 7,500 km (4,660 miles) and its landscapes vary from north to south. It is from the Northeast, home to beaches such as Taipus de Fora, Bahia (pictured), that paradise-like images of picturesque white sand lapped by aquamarine seas and backed by swaying palms originate.

RIGHT The Brazilian territory that sits on the Amazon Basin is known as "*Amazônia Legal*" (Legal Amazon) and comprises no less than nine states. According to the 2010 census, 24 million people live in this area — with only an estimated 250,000 of indigenous origin.

ABOVE The proximity of Trancoso to the vibrant tourist magnet Porto Seguro, further north, put the small village on the map in the 1990s. More recently, large international resorts and boutique hotels have opened their doors here, attracting national and foreign celebrities every year.

TOP Located in the area where the first Portuguese explorers disembarked when they discovered Brazil; Trancoso, Bahia, was founded in 1586 by Jesuit priests. The main church and small houses from those days remain standing in the centre of the village, in an area known as "*O Quadrado*" (the square).

ABOVE With 932 km (579 miles) of coastline, the state of Bahia draws tourists from all over the country and abroad. Add to this a beautiful and energetic capital city, Salvador (pictured), a rich African heritage reflected in its music and its food and a well-organized touristic infrastructure, and you have one of Brazil's most-loved destinations.

RIGHT One of the most peculiar landscapes in the country, the Lençóis Maranhenses National Park is an extensive system of large sweeping dunes dotted with blue lagoons. Formed during the rainy season and disappearing in the dry season, the lagoons are home to a variety of fish whose eggs are transported from the sea by birds.

OPPOSITE Located in the state of Maranhão, the Lençóis Maranhenses belong to the ecosystem known as Cerrado (savannah). To explore its 155,000 hectares (383,000 acres), tourists can fly from the capital city of São Luís to Barreirinhas, on its doorway, or take a more romantic route down the Preguiças River.

RIGHT Pipa, near Natal, in the state of Rio Grande do Norte, is one of the most famous beaches of Brazil. It became a popular destination after being discovered by surfers and backpackers in the 1970s. The 10-metre (33-foot) vertical cliffs and the remnants of native Atlantic Forest mark the landscape.

BELOW The waterfall of Pedra Branca (white rock) on the outskirts of Paraty, in the state of Rio de Janeiro, is one of the hidden gems of the exuberant Atlantic Forest. Made up of dense, tree-covered mountains, wetland and tropical islands, this ecosystem stretches along Brazil's west coastline and contains one of the planet's highest concentrations of biodiversity.

LEFT It is virtually impossible to talk about Rio de Janeiro and not refer to its beautiful beaches. From the world-famous sands of Copacabana and Ipanema (pictured) to the more secluded Urca and Joatinga, *cariocas* (Rio natives) pick their favourite spot in the sun and make beach culture a lifestyle.

BELOW LEFT Although Rio enjoys warm temperatures all year round, it is in summer that *cariocas* make the most of the city's natural wonders. Here, residents go for a night dip at the trendy Arpoador Beach.

RIGHT The fishing village of Jericoacoara, Ceará, was never the same after tourists from across the globe discovered it in the mid-1980s. Its endless dunes, crystal-clear waters and interestingly shaped rocks were turned into a National Park in 2002.

BELOW RIGHT Blessed by year-round temperatures that vary between 23 and 30°C (73 and 86°F), the coastline of the Ceará state is one of Brazil's most sought-after destinations. Its capital city, Fortaleza, receives around half a million tourists annually. Many carry on to explore the surrounding near-deserted beaches and sand dunes.

ABOVE One of the country's finest coastal settings is the ecotourism jewel of Fernando de Noronha, located 350 km (217 miles) off the coast of Natal. Twenty-one islands make up this picturesque archipelago, which is renowned worldwide for its coral reefs teeming with marine life.

ABOVE A shoal of sardines in the sea at Fernando de Noronha. The crystal-clear waters make for some of Brazil's best diving. Around 230 species of fish are among the star attractions of the archipelago.

ABOVE The magnificent beaches of Fernando de Noronha are always free from crowds, as limited flights keep visitor numbers to under 350 per day.

ABOVE Located on the island of Santa Catarina, Florianópolis has dozens of exquisite beaches, as well as a few lagoons. Popular with surfers since the 1970s, the Joaquina Beach (pictured) today attracts a crowd of fans of other sports.

ABOVE AND RIGHT The Saint Peter and Saint Paul
Archipelago is a group of 15 small islands and rocks
located some 1,000 km (621 miles) from Natal. It is
controlled by the Brazilian Navy, which maintains a
scientific station in the area. The rocks are inhabited
by birds such as brown boobies and brown and black
noddies, with other wildlife including crabs and spiders.

ABOVE AND RIGHT Not far from the coast of Rio de
Janeiro, Ilha Grande (big island) was for a long time
viewed as the ideal location for isolating political prisoners
and highly dangerous criminals. When the prison was
demolished in 1994, Brazilians rediscovered a well-
preserved tract of Atlantic rainforest, with many waterfalls
and more than 100 beaches.

RIGHT Located in the Northeast, the Caatinga covers over 10 per cent of Brazil's territory and is known for its semi-arid climate. The ecosystem is home to endemic bird and reptile species, which, alongside its 15 million inhabitants, are vulnerable to severe droughts, such as the one registered in 2012 in places including Filadélfia, Bahia (pictured).

LEFT Some 275 individual cascades, 80 m (262 ft) high and 3 km (9,842 ft) wide, create in Iguaçú one of the world's most awe-inspiring waterfalls. Subtropical rainforest surrounds the falls and is home to a wide variety of plant and animal life.

OPPOSITE Spread between Brazil and Argentina, the thundering Iguaçu waterfalls have long enchanted visitors. Hundreds of years before Europeans first visited the area, Tupi-Guarani tribes used the falls as a sacred burial ground – in Guarani, the name *Iguaçu* means "great waters".

OPPOSITE The Iguaçu National Park, in the state of Paraná, was created in 1939 and is home to a large remaining portion of the Atlantic Forest, inhabited by tapirs, giant anteaters, howler monkeys, toucans (pictured), macaws and harpy eagles. Because of its diversity, it has been declared a UNESCO Heritage Site.

RIGHT Around 2,000 species of vascular plant can be found in the forests surrounding the Iguaçu Falls, in an area that spreads over 400,000 hectares (988,422 acres), across Brazil and in Argentina. At night, the Southern Cross and Magellanic Clouds (pictured, left) are easily visible, as is the bright star Sirius (right).

BOTTOM RIGHT Endemic to the Caatinga and Cerrado ecosystems, the Brazilian three-banded armadillo (*Tolypeutes tricinctus*) is one of the only two species of armadillo that can roll into a ball. This feature inspired the mascot of the 2014 World Cup, named Fuleco.

ABOVE AND OPPOSITE The Pantanal wetland offer even better opportunities for wildlife watching than the dense foliage of the Amazon. Although *pantano* means swamp in Portuguese, this is not a swamp but rather a vast alluvial plain, comprising grassy savannah, forests and meadows, forming a unique habitat for animals including Jabiru storks (above) and giant otters (opposite top).

ABOVE Many species found in the Amazon are also to be spotted in the Pantanal, including the fearsome jaguar *Panthera onca*. Though classified as vulnerable by the environmental authorities, in rural areas creatures that threaten livestock may be hunted.

TOP RIGHT An emerald hummingbird hovers in the air by flapping its wings 12–90 times per second in order to drink the nectar from flowers.

BOTTOM RIGHT According to UNESCO, the Pantanal is home to some 650 species of bird, such as the Chestnut-eared Araçari (*Pteroglossus castanotis*). Ibis, herons and egrets wade along the shoreline, while black-collared hawks and enormous hyacinth macaws soar overhead.

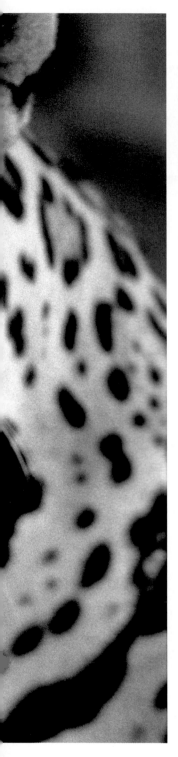

LEFT The Formoso River is one of many tributaries to the Paraguay River which snake around the city of Bonito. The region is part of the Serra da Bodoquena National Park and attracts tourists with its waterfalls, caves and lagoons.

BELOW The town of Bonito, in Mato Grosso do Sul, is not billed as the Caribbean of the Centre-West for nothing. Due to the large quantity of limestone in the ground, the rivers around the city are a clear blue, giving snorkellers an enviable view of its aquatic life. Bonito is one of the hottest eco-tourism destinations in Brazil, so the local government has been imposing restrictive measures to ensure its sustainable development.

RIGHT A macaw in the Mato Grosso do Sul region, which translates as "thick forest of the south".

BELOW Guira cuckoos roost on a branch. This distinctive looking bird, native to eastern and southern Brazil, gives off an unpleasant smell due to its large anal glands, unique to its species, *Crotophaginae*.

LEFT The interior of Brazil conjures up the magic of outback travel, with big skies, jagged canyons and sandstone hills rolling across the plains. The Chapada dos Guimarães, in Mato Grosso state, with its naturally formed *Cidade de Pedra* (stone city) (pictured) is the unofficial geographic centre of South America.

LEFT The *Véu de Noiva* (bride's veil) waterfall in Chapada dos Guimarães. Scattered across several of the country's hinterland states, the *chapadas* are geological formations of steeply carved sandstone cliffs ranging in elevation from 800–2,000 m (2,625–6,562 ft) above sea level.

ABOVE The native vegetation of the Cerrado has about 10,000 plant species, some exclusive to the region, such as the *sempre-viva* (*Paepalanthus bromelioides*). Despite its invaluable natural treasures, only 1.5 per cent of the ecosystem is under the protection of Federal Reserves, such as the Serra da Canastra National Park, in Minas Gerais (pictured).

TOP Spreading through the Central-West region of Brazil and occupying 21 per cent of the country's land, the Cerrado is a savannah rich in biodiversity. More than 800 species of bird are believed to live in the area, among them the flightless Greater Rhea (*Rhea americana*), Brazil's largest bird.

ABOVE In the northeastern state of Bahia, the Chapada Diamantina is a tourist attraction in its own right. A vast region of valleys and plateaux, waterfalls and crisp mountains, it takes its name from the diamonds found here in the nineteenth century.

FROM BAROQUE CATHEDRALS TO HIGH MODERNISM

Brazil's architectural heritage has been shaped by its European roots and its openness to bold ideas from abroad, as well as the landscape itself – verdant forests, tropical setting and vast open spaces have all been a great source of inspiration over the last 300 years.

The Portuguese left a deep and lasting imprint on Brazil. Salvador, in the Northeast, served as the capital from 1549–1763, and its beautifully preserved historic centre is lined with colourful colonial buildings and baroque churches. The 1723 Church of São Francisco is one of Brazil's greatest examples, with an exuberant interior filled with ornate woodcarvings and abundant use of gold detailing.

During the gold rush of the eighteenth century, the mineral-rich mountains of present-day Minas Gerais transformed dusty mining towns into grand centres of art and architecture. Ouro Preto is the finest of the bunch, with hilly cobblestone streets crowded with colonial buildings and magnificent churches. The eighteenth-century Church of Santa Efigênia dos Pretos was built by and for the black slave community and largely financed by Chico Rei, an enslaved African tribal king who managed to buy his freedom and eventually liberate his entire tribe sometime in the 1700s. The images of black saints inside the church were objects of great devotion to slaves, who prayed they would survive the brutal working conditions in the mines.

Like a number of other churches in the region,

Santa Efigênia dos Pretos contains carvings by the master sculptor and architect Antônio Francisco Lisboa, better known as O *Aleijadinho* (the little cripple) for the disease – probably leprosy – that debilitated him. After losing his fingers and toes and the use of his lower legs, he had to be carried to work sites by his assistants but that didn't stop Lisboa (who was the son of a Portuguese architect and a black slave). He strapped chisels and hammers to his arms and continued sculpting, developing a unique, exquisite style of carving that adorns the churches in and around Ouro Preto. His masterpiece is O*s Profetas* (the prophets), 12 magnificent sculptures depicting biblical characters artfully arranged before the Basílica do Bom Jesus de Matosinhos in Congonhas.

The arrival of the Portuguese royalty to their New World colony had a dramatic impact on the design of Brazilian cities in the nineteenth century. Nowhere was this more evident than in Rio de Janeiro, which was declared the capital of the United Kingdom of Portugal, Brazil and the Algarves in 1815. The Portuguese King Dom João VI helped transform a grubby backwater into a splendid European-style municipality and the seat of an empire. With no lodging suitable for a king, a rich merchant named Elias Antônio Lopes donated his manor house and estate, which was embellished and expanded to the extent that the new Quinta da Boa Vista palace became known as "tropical Versailles".

Despite the invasion of Portugal by Napoleon in

1807, the king was a lover of all things French. He invited an artistic mission of architects, artists and artisans from France to help remake the city. The Neoclassical style then in vogue throughout Europe came to dominate the new capital, with the great Parisian architect Auguste-Henri-Victor Grandjean de Montigny (1776–1850) playing a pivotal role in the development of Brazilian architecture. De Montigny, who settled in Brazil in 1822 and spent the rest of his life there, designed his own home (the magnificent Solar Grandjean de Montigny, today part of the Pontifical Catholic University of Rio), the edifice for the Praça do Comércio (which today houses the Casa França-Brasil cultural centre) and the Imperial Academy of Fine Arts, of which only the portico remains.

Over the next century, Brazilian designers continued to embrace European ideas and, like France, Brazil entered its own *Belle Époque* from the 1860s to the early 1900s. Neoclassical style, which favoured grandiose, monumental works referencing Ancient Greece and Rome, remained quite popular, both in Rio and throughout Brazil. Key buildings from the time include the lavish Theatro da Paz (opened in 1874) in Belém, a city located near the mouth of the Amazon River. A few years later, in 1896, the Neo-Renaissance Teatro Amazonas opened in Manaus, boasting a similarly extravagant design: some 36,000 ceramic tiles, painted in the colours of the Brazilian flag, cover its domed roof. With wealth flooding in from the rubber boom, no expense was spared, and most of the materials — Italian marble and glass, Scottish cast iron — came from Europe. Manaus' municipal market, completed in 1883 (and still standing today), was a copy of the famed Les Halles in Paris.

At the turn of the twentieth century Brazil went through a period of modernization that brought exciting changes to urban design. Rio's streets were widened and grand boulevards created, with Avenida Rio Branco becoming the city's Champs-Elysées. The magnificent Theatro Municipal (completed in 1909), modelled on the Le Palais Garnier in Paris, opened in Rio and dazzled audiences with sculpture, mosaics and paintings by some of Brazil's most important artists of the time, including Eliseu Visconti (1866-1944). As in many other parts of the industrialized world, the 1920s were boom days and Art Deco arrived in full force with the opening of Rio's Hotel Glória and Copacabana Palace (1923). In 1926, construction began on the Christ the Redeemer statue, considered the largest Art Deco monument in the world, though it would not be completed until 1931 — a time marked by worldwide depression (and the collapse of Brazil's booming coffee market) that would bring profound changes to many facets of society, including urban design.

The 1930s saw the emergence of a new generation of Brazilian architects, who were interested in the ideas of Modernism sweeping across the world and also dedicated to forging a uniquely Brazilian style. The first seeds of this new paradigm — that included not only architecture, but art, music and literature — were planted in 1927, when the Russo-Brazilian architect Gregori Warchavchik (1896–1972) built the first Modernist building in São Paulo. Famous Swiss-born architect Le Corbusier (1887–1965) gave a further boost to an incipient group of Modernist Brazilian architects when he visited Brazil in 1929. Le Corbusier proved influential on two rising stars in the architecture world. Lúcio Costa (1902–98) and Oscar Niemeyer (1907–2012), who would achieve worldwide fame for their utopian design of Brasília, a city created from scratch in under four years in the

midst of an empty unpopulated stretch of countryside.

Brasília, which became the nation's new capital when it was completed in 1960, is still considered one of the world's boldest urban designs. Its unusual shape, compared to an airplane or a bird in flight, and its masterfully planned grid at the time represented a futuristic vision of what cities could aspire to. Niemeyer designed many iconic buildings for the capital, including the crown-like Catedral Metropolitana, with its curved, slender columns, and the blindingly white government buildings of the Praça dos Trés Poderes (Plaza of Three Powers), which house the three key branches of government: the Palácio do Planalto (Presidential Planalto Palace), the Congresso Nacional (National Congress) and the Supremo Tribunal Federal (Supreme Federal Court).

Niemeyer had a long and celebrated career, designing scores of buildings both in Brazil and abroad (as a leftist and critic of the military dictatorship, he fled the country in 1964 and lived in Paris until 1985). Many of his buildings eschew the right angle in favour of sensuous curves and elegant geometry. He died just 10 days shy of his 105th birthday, and his influence on architecture — not only in Brazil, but also across the globe — was profound.

Many other talented Brazilian architects emerged during the latter half of the twentieth century and they helped to create a unique vernacular of Brazilian Modernist design. Rome-born Lina Bo Bardi (1914–1992) emigrated to Brazil after World War II and went on to become one of the country's most famous female architects. Her Casa de Vidro (Glass House), built in São Paulo in 1951, consists of a framed rectangular cube delicately perched atop slender columns that blend into the surrounding landscape. She continued to explore notions of space and absence in avant-garde designs such as the Museu de Arte de São Paulo (Art Museum of São Paulo), featuring a giant red concrete frame that suspends the interior glass structure above the ground.

Paulo Mendes da Rocha was awarded the Pritzker Prize (the Nobel of the architecture world) in 2006

for an innovative body of work, which has helped revitalize his hometown city of São Paulo. One of his best-known projects was the redesign of the Pinacoteca do Estado de São Paulo, one of Brazil's most important art galleries.

As Brazil embraced Modernism, and the country became increasingly urban, more and more people migrated to the cities in search of work. Those without means often ended up in *favelas*, poor makeshift communities (often described as "slums") built on unoccupied lands. Favelas have been around since the late 1800s, though they began to grow exponentially from the 1970s onwards. For years, government policy was simply to ignore or bulldoze them out of existence, but in recent years they have merited greater attention from both the municipal and federal government.

According to the latest (2010) census around 6 per cent of Brazilians (over 11 million people) live in favelas. Government investment has brought improvements to some of them — such as Rio's Complexo do Alemão, where an aerial tram provides speedy (and scenic) transportation for residents who once had to walk long distances through narrow streets in order to reach a bus or train station. Other favelas have seen noticeable improvements in security, health and sanitation, also education as government funds add city services to once-neglected communities. There is still a long way to go, however, with millions living in crowded, unsanitary conditions, where crime, pollution, malnutrition and disease are all too common.

International artists have sought to bring positive change to the favelas. Santa Marta in Rio de Janeiro has several dozen residences painted in vibrant rainbow colours, courtesy of Dutch artists Jeroen Koolhaas and Dre Urhahn, known as Haas & Hahn. In nearby Morro da Providência, the oversized portraits created by French artist JR have helped to show a more humane, individual side of the *favela* opposed to that of a faceless million-plus who inhabit Rio's shanty towns.

PREVIOUS PAGE The Portuguese left a deep and lasting legacy on Brazil. Salvador, in the Northeast, served as the capital from 1549–1763, and its beautifully preserved historic centre is lined with colourful colonial buildings and baroque churches. It is known for its African heritage, an influence apparent in the local cuisine and music.

ABOVE Founded at the end of the seventeenth century, when the state of Minas Gerais was first explored for its gold reserves, Ouro Preto was Brazil's first city to be declared a UNESCO World Heritage Site. The Portuguese imprint can be seen on the town's many colonial buildings and baroque churches.

ABOVE During the gold rush of the eighteenth century, dusty mining towns were transformed into grand centres of art and architecture. Often shadowed by its neighbour Ouro Preto, the city of Mariana also has much to offer when it comes to Brazilian colonial art, such as the churches of St Francis of Assisi (left) and Our Lady of the Assumption (right).

ABOVE The Basílica do Senhor Bom Jesus de Matosinhos, in Congonhas do Campo, Minas Gerais. The 12 soapstone sculptures shown here, named "The Prophets", depict biblical characters and are masterpieces carved by Antônio Francisco Lisboa. Known as "*O Aleijadinho*" (the little cripple), due to a degenerative disease that caused him to lose his fingers and toes, Lisboa created the most celebrated artworks of Brazilian baroque.

TOP Founded in the sixteenth century during the sugar boom in Pernambuco, Olinda is the second Brazilian city to become a World Heritage Site. The town is known for its beautiful churches and its *carnaval*, when thousands gather to dance and celebrate to the tunes of local rhythms, *frevo* and *maracatu*.

ABOVE Originally a convent and then the customs house of the busy port of Recife, the capital of Pernambuco, this 1732 building today hosts a shopping facility in the regenerated historic centre. Founded in the sixteenth century, the city enjoyed a rich period when the state was one of the main producers of sugar. Its architecture is also influenced by a brief period under the control of the Dutch empire, who occupied Pernambuco in 1630.

ABOVE The black community of slaves and former slaves of Bahia were devoted to Our Lady of the Rosary, and in 1704 their brotherhood gathered enough money to erect their own church, in the district of Pelourinho, in Salvador. Shown here, the building mirrors the style of the time and is decorated with typical Portuguese *azulejos* (ceramic tiles).

ABOVE During Brazil's colonial period, many fortresses were built along its coasts. Building commenced on The Forte dos Reis Magos (The Three Kings Fortress) two years before the city of Natal was founded, in 1598. It is shaped as a polygon, in the typical manner of military buildings in the sixteenth century.

ABOVE Although founded by French explorers, São Luís, the capital of the state of Maranhão, was soon re-taken by the Portuguese in 1615. It is another example of the emblematic architecture of the sixteenth to eighteenth centuries. Nowadays, the town is also known as Brazil's reggae capital and home to a rich cultural heritage, combining Indigenous and African influences.

RIGHT The arrival of the Portuguese royalty in Brazil in 1808 had a dramatic impact on the design of its cities. King Dom João VI was a lover of all things French, an influence that would remain until the early twentieth century. In Manaus, capital of the state of Amazonas, the municipal market, completed in 1883 and still standing today, is a copy of the famed Les Halles in Paris.

LEFT AND ABOVE Opened in Manaus in 1896, the
neo-Renaissance Teatro Amazonas is an icon of the
prosperity generated by the rubber boom. Some 36,000
ceramic tiles, painted in the colours of the Brazilian flag,
cover its domed roof. Most of the materials – Italian marble
and glass, Scottish cast iron – came from Europe.

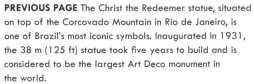

PREVIOUS PAGE The Christ the Redeemer statue, situated on top of the Corcovado Mountain in Rio de Janeiro, is one of Brazil's most iconic symbols. Inaugurated in 1931, the 38 m (125 ft) statue took five years to build and is considered to be the largest Art Deco monument in the world.

ABOVE Modelled on the Palais Garnier in Paris, the Theatro Municipal opened in Rio de Janeiro in 1909, with sculpture, mosaics and paintings from some of Brazil's leading artists of the day, including Eliseu Visconti (1866–1944). This symbol of Rio's glamorous past is part of Cinelândia Square's architectural set, along with the National Library and the Fine Arts Museum.

RIGHT As in many other parts of the industrialized world, the 1920s were boom days, and Art Deco arrived in Brazil in full force with the opening of Rio's Copacabana Palace Hotel (1923). Inspired by hotels on the French Riviera, the *Copa* (as *cariocas* call it) is still the ultimate luxury destination, having received such illustrious guests as Diana, Princess of Wales, Nelson Mandela, Walt Disney and Mick Jagger.

OPPOSITE At the beginning of the twentieth century, the Rua XV de Novembro (15 November Street) was regarded as one of the most sophisticated thoroughfares of São Paulo, a symbol of the city's wealth generated by the coffee boom. At the time, most of the town's commerce, banks, newspapers, hotels, cafés and cigar shops were concentrated there. Now it is a pedestrian street, packed with popular shops.

RIGHT Often seen as an intimidating concrete jungle, São Paulo compensates for its lack of natural beauty with a rich cultural life and a lively gastronomic scene. The wide array of museums and galleries and award winning restaurants of several world cuisines reflect the various immigrants who have made their home in the city.

RIGHT The Altino Arantes Building (pictured, back left) was inspired by the Empire State Building in New York. From the 1930s onward, Brazil witnessed the emergence of a new generation of architects. An incipient group of Modernist Brazilians received a boost after a visit to the country by Swiss-born master Le Corbusier. São Paulo would then become the home of several daring Modernist buildings, still seen scattered around the city, buildings, such as the Edifício Copan, designed by Oscar Niemeyer, and Lina Bo Bardi's MASP (Museu de Arte de São Paulo).

LEFT Lúcio Costa and Oscar Niemeyer achieved worldwide fame for their utopian design of Brasília, a city created from scratch in under four years in the midst of an empty, unpopulated stretch of countryside. The imposing National Congress building is one among several iconic buildings in the Brazilian capital.

RIGHT Brasília became Brazil's new capital once it was completed in 1960 and it is still considered to be one of the world's boldest urban designs. The 33 m (108 ft) high, 60 m (197 ft) diameter conical Cathedral of Brasília is one of several renowned buildings in the city designed by architect Oscar Niemeyer. The ground-breaking took place in 1958 and the construction was finished in 1960, but was not officially opened until 1970.

ABOVE The Museum of Contemporary Art in Niterói, close
to Rio de Janeiro, became the source of the city's greatest
pride and its most iconic symbol after it opened in 1996.
Some compare its shape to that of a flying saucer. It is yet
another example of Niemeyer's daring futuristic design.

TOP The Memorial dos Povos Indígenas (Memorial of Indigenous Peoples) , Brasília. A key figure in the development of modern architecture, Oscar Niemeyer often claimed that the female form and the geography of Brazil were the main source of inspiration for the curves that often feature in his work.

BELOW Designed by Oscar Niemeyer in 1958, Brasília's Palácio da Alvorada is the official presidential residence. Its name, meaning "Palace of Dawn", was given by the first Brazilian leader to reside there, Juscelino Kubitschek.

ABOVE The Ibirapuera Auditorium in São Paulo is one of Niemeyer's projects that precedes the construction of Brasília, but bears the architect's main trademarks, with its reinforced concrete structure. Niemeyer remained a staunch communist throughout most of his life and was forced into exile during Brazil's military rule in the 1960s.

ABOVE A few years after having returned from space, Soviet cosmonaut Yuri Gagarin visited Brasília and said he felt as if he was visiting another planet. That is often the impression left by Oscar Niemeyer's characteristic style, displayed in works such as Niterói's Teatro Popular (people's theatre), which opened next to the Museum of Contemporary Art in 2007. It was one of the last works of Niemeyer to be inaugurated in Brazil.

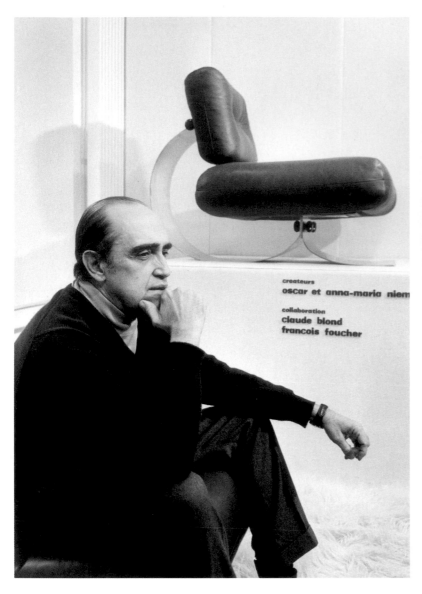

ABOVE Oscar Niemeyer (pictured here in 1977) died in 2012, at the age of 104, and carried on designing new projects until his last days. *The New York Times* defined him as the man "whose flowing designs infused Modernism with a new sensuality and captured the imaginations of generations of architects around the world".

RIGHT The Copan building (left) is one of the grand projects that Oscar Niemeyer devised for São Paulo ahead of the city's 400th anniversary, celebrated in 1954. Due to the collapse of one of the financing institutions, the construction was only completed in 1957. It remains one of the city's most iconic landmarks.

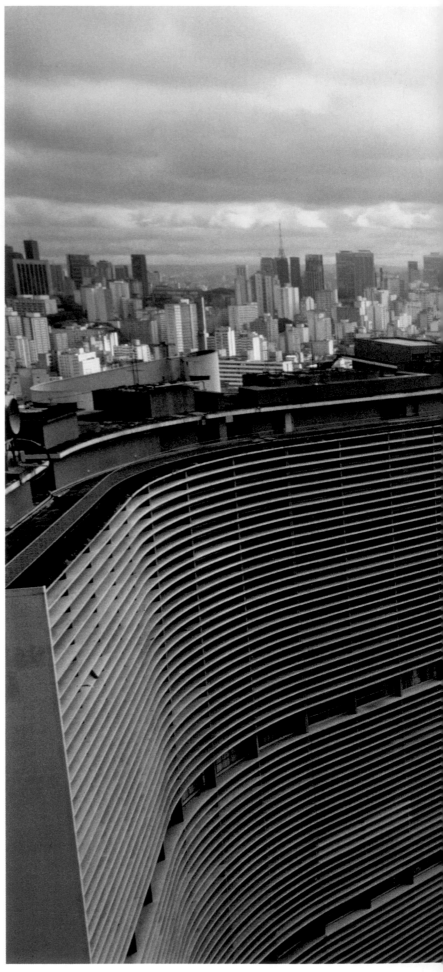

LEFT Paulo Mendes da Rocha (1928–) was awarded the Pritzker Prize in 2006 for an innovative body of work, which has helped revitalize São Paulo. One of his best-known projects was the redesign of the Pinacoteca do Estado de São Paulo (pictured), one of Brazil's most important art galleries.

BELOW São Paulo's Museum of Art (MASP) is one of the city's most visited attractions. It was designed in 1968 by Italo-Brazilian Modernist architect Lina Bo Bardi (1914–1992), famed for exploring notions of space and absence. The museum is renowned for its peculiar shape, featuring a giant red concrete frame that suspends the interior glass structure above the ground.

RIGHT Born in 1952, Isay Weinfeld is one of Brazil's leading contemporary architects, whose works include this Modernist house, as well as the renowned Hotel Fasano and the Havaianas store, both in São Paulo. He has a diverse portfolio, having also designed furniture, as well as sets for theatre and cinema.

BELOW São Paulo's Octávio Frias de Oliveira Bridge is a 138 m (453 ft) tall, cable-stayed bridge spanning 1.6 km (0.10 miles) over the Pinheiros River, in the city's new business district. Designed by João Valente Filho (1949–2011), It is considered an architectural wonder owing to its unique shape, with two tracks forming a "X" supported by a single concrete mast. During the evening, its cables are lit up in different colours.

ABOVE A bridge designed by Oscar Niemeyer in the vicinity of Brazil's largest shantytown, Rocinha, in Rio. With between 60,000 to 150,000 residents, it was once a neighbourhood where drug traffickers and armed gangs acted freely. Like other shantytowns in the city, it has recently undergone a police-led operation to allow the state authorities to regain full control over the territory.

OPPOSITE As the country became increasingly urban, more and more people migrated to the cities in search of work. Those without means often ended up in *favelas*, poor makeshift communities (often described as slums), built on unoccupied lands, such as Gamboa in Rio (pictured here in 1955).

RIGHT Vertical slums, such as the São Vito building, in São Paulo, became a problem in the centre of big cities in the 1980s, as middle-class families moved to the suburbs. Known as *Treme-Treme* (Shiver-Shiver) for housing around 3,000 people in the 1980s, the São Vito was expropriated in 2004 and demolished in 2011.

LEFT A boy walks through the alleyways of Santa Marta, a *favela* in Rio de Janeiro, a few days after the setting up of a Peacemaking Police Unit, in 2011. The force intends to prevent drug trafficking, especially in the southern zone of Rio, where extreme violence makes international news.

ABOVE *Favelas*, such as Rio's Rocinha, have been around since the late 1800s, although they began to grow exponentially from the 1970s onward. For years, government policy was simply to ignore or bulldoze them out of existence, but in recent years they have merited greater attention from both the municipal and federal government.

OPPOSITE TOP According to the 2010 census, over 11 million Brazilians live in *favelas*. In Manaus, capital of the state of Amazonas and home to over 2,2 million people, many shantytowns are made up of *palafitas* (stilt houses) that sit over the Negro River.

OPPOSITE BELOW In Rio, government investment has brought improvements to some of the *favelas*. In Complexo do Alemão, an aerial tram provides speedy transportation for residents who once had to walk long distances through narrow streets in order to reach a bus or train station.

RIGHT Few places in the world combine nature and urban life as Rio de Janeiro. Breathtaking views, such as the famous Copacabana Beach and the Sugarloaf Mountain, have helped earn the city recognition as a UNESCO World Heritage Site. Brazilians simply prefer to call it *Cidade Maravilhosa* (the Marvellous City).

ABOVE AND RIGHT Belo Horizonte, capital of Minas Gerais and Brazil's third largest city, was designed in the 1890s by two Brazilian urban planners, Aarão Reis and Francisco Bicalho, who took inspiration from Washington, D.C. In the early 1940s, under then mayor Juscelino Kubitschek, the man-made lagoon of Pampulha was built. Surrounding it is a group of buildings designed by Oscar Niemeyer, most notably the Church of St Francis of Assisi (right).

ABOVE The second largest city in the Amazon, Belém, in the state of Pará, sits on the entrance gate to the Amazon River. Once part of this busy port, the Estação das Docas (Docklands) underwent a restoration process in 2000 that saw its abandoned early twentieth-century warehouses transformed into a leisure area complete with restaurants, bars and shops.

ABOVE One of Brazil's most popular tourist destinations, Natal, in Rio Grande do Norte, is blessed with sunny and warm weather, magnificent beaches and the estuary of the Potengi River (pictured). But as with many other capital cities in the country, it is experiencing rapid growth and is now home to over 1.2 million people.

ABOVE The Lacerda Elevator is the most recognizable
landmark of Salvador, capital of the state of Bahia.
Inaugurated in 1873, it links the Cidade Baixa (lower city),
in the vicinity of the port, to the Cidade Alta (higher city),
the town's business heart. Salvador is one of the cities that
will host the 2014 World Cup.

ABOVE The fifth largest city in Brazil, Fortaleza, the capital city of Ceará, impresses visitors with its sandy beaches and cultural heritage. Colonization began in the seventeenth century but grew during a brief cotton boom of the nineteenth century. Today, the metropolitan region is home to almost 3.4 million.

ABOVE The bus rapid transit system (BRT) is a trademark of Curitiba, capital city of Paraná. It was developed by a team led by architect Jaime Lerner (1937–) in the 1960s as part of a major urban design planned to cope with the town's growing population. Lerner later became mayor in three different periods, and Curitiba is today considered to be one of the world's best examples of urban planning.

ABOVE A view of Hercílio Luz Bridge, Brazil's longest
suspension bridge, linking the mainland to the city of
Florianópolis, on Santa Catarina island. Colonized by
settlers from the Azores and Madeira in the 1740s, today
it has over 1 million inhabitants, who enjoy a high quality
of life. *Floripa*, as it is called, is the Brazilian capital city
with the highest Human Development Index score,
according to the UN.

NATURAL RESOURCES & THE RISE OF MODERN BRAZIL

Blessed with abundant natural resources, Brazil has seen its fortunes rise over the past generation due to an economic boom fuelled by a wide range of sectors including agriculture, mining, petroleum, hydroelectric energy, manufacturing and biofuels. Up until the twentieth century, the economy was one of boom and bust, its prosperity and privation often tied to the dominant produce of the time – from Brazilwood (harvested by early Portuguese colonists in the 1500s) and sugarcane (1600s), to gold (1700s), rubber (1890–1920) and coffee (1880–1930). Economic crises once dogged the economy, as did hyperinflation: from the time when Brazil became a republic in 1889 until Fernando Henrique Cardoso (1931–) became president in 1995, Brazil had a cumulative inflation rate of over a quadrillion per cent. In more recent years a dramatic turnaround has been experienced, and today it has one of the most balanced and diversified economies in the world.

PETROLEUM

Brazil has come a long way since the discovery of commercially viable oil fields, back in the 1930s. Throughout the 1940s, the country still imported over 90 per cent of its oil. There was great hope, however, that abundant reserves were yet to be found and, tapping into popular sentiment, President Getúlio Vargas created Petrobras, an oil company owned and run by the state with exclusive rights in drilling for gas and oil. The tactic would prove extremely fortuitous,

although when Petrobras began operations in 1954, it was pumping under 3,000 barrels per day – meeting less than 3 per cent of Brazil's energy needs at the time. It wasn't until Brazil began offshore explorations in the 1970s that its luck began to change. In 1974, discoveries were made all along the coastline, to such an extent that Petrobras had to relinquish its monopoly in order to effectively exploit the many sites. Within a decade, Brazil was producing over 500,000 barrels a day – a huge leap from years past, but still not enough to meet growing energy needs. Meanwhile, Petrobras continued to grow, eventually expanding to 24 other countries including the USA, Portugal and Japan, and diversifying into the realms of electricity and biofuel.

In 2006 Brazil achieved self-sufficiency in crude oil. At that time Petrobras was producing two million barrels of oil a day, and proven reserves stood at eight billion barrels. New finds, however, have added to the Brazilian cache – including staggering oil fields 300 km (186 miles) offshore that could contain as much as 30 billion barrels of oil. New technologies will be required – necessitating tens of thousands of new workers – to successfully develop the reserves, which are at a depth that presents enormous logistical and environmental challenges.

Petrobras remains on a sound financial footing. As Brazil's largest company and biggest taxpayer, it has over 80,000 employees and a market value in excess of US$290 billion, making

it the world's sixth biggest company according to market value.

BIOFUELS

Petroleum is only part of the picture when it comes to Brazil's energy success story. The development and growth of the biofuel industry is yet another of the nation's significant achievements. Sugarcane – one of the oldest commercial crops in the country – has turned out, remarkably, to be a sustainable, energy-efficient fuel source when converted into ethyl alcohol (better known as ethanol). After the oil crisis of 1973, Brazil began developing its ethanol industry. The government, then a military dictatorship, wanted to reduce the country's dependence on foreign oil.

During the 1970s, the government invested heavily in the biofuel program, providing subsidies to sugar producers and incentivizing automobile manufacturers to make cars with engines that ran on ethanol. Throughout the 1980s and 90s, the program experienced ups and downs – the latter when surging sugarcane prices made ethanol more expensive than petrol and thus less desirable to motorists and consequently manufacturers. The big break, however, came in 2003, when engineers developed new "flex-fuel" engines, which were able to run on ethanol, petrol or any combination of the two. As a result, ethanol today accounts for about half of all fuel sales, and even regular petrol contains a 25 per cent mixture of ethanol. The flex-fuel engine has also

ABOVE A worker sieves harvested Arabica coffee beans at Ponto Alegre farm in Cabo Verde, Minas Gerais. The state is Brazil's largest producer of coffee, contributing to more than half the country's total output. Brazilians are the top global exporters of the product and, in recent years, have also become one of the biggest consumer nations.

LEFT A Yanomami woman prepares manioc. Manioc, or cassava, is cultivated for its edible, starchy root. It is one of the largest sources of carbohydrate in the tropics, but it contains few other nutritients and when improperly treated the roots and leaves can produce cyanide.

LEFT A rural worker picks up dry coconut rind to use its fibres to make man-made materials at a family farm in Ceará-Mirim, some 31 miles (50 km) northeast of Natal.

ABOVE In recent years, government and non-governmental organizations have created extractive reserves in the Amazon to be used by locals who depend on subsistence agriculture and traditional extractive activities, such as rubber tapping, fishing, fruit or nut collecting (pictured here near Belém, Pará). Increasingly, these reserves are seen as playing a key role in the preservation of the forest.

ABOVE Favourable weather conditions allow farmers in the Central-West of Brazil to produce a second harvest each year, generally of corn, cotton or sorghum. The so-called *safrinha* (small harvest) is also helped by the adoption of sustainable practices such as no-till farming and crop-livestock integration.

RIGHT An Embraer EMB 202 Ipanema agricultural aircraft crop spraying a cotton field. Brazil is the world's fifth largest producer of the crop. Between 2010 and 2011 the annual harvest increased by over 50 per cent.

TOP Southern Brazil, with its cooler climate and dry mountainous landscape, proved an excellent wine-growing region. In the nineteenth century, Italian immigrants planted many of the vineyards that flourish in the soils of Rio Grande do Sul and Santa Catarina (pictured), where dozens of wineries produce more than 12 million bottles a year.

ABOVE A worker plants eucalyptus at the Eldorado Celulose e Papel seedling nursery in Andradina, in the state of São Paulo. Today, 100 per cent of Brazil's paper and pulp production comes from the country's planted forests of pine trees and eucalyptus, scattered around the Southeast and Central Regions.

LEFT Combines harvest soybeans at the Morro Azul farm near Tangará da Serra, Mato Grosso. Heavy investment in research and technology over the past 50 years boosted Brazil's grain output by more than 700 per cent, while only doubling the amount of land used for crops.

ABOVE An importer of food until the 1970s, Brazil is now the world's third largest exporter of agricultural goods, behind the US and the EU. Production of soybeans in places such as Correntina, Bahia (pictured), has played an enormous role in the sector's growth. The main buyer of Brazilian soy is China.

ABOVE Orange juice is another big player in Brazil's exports portfolio. The country is the world's largest producer and exporter of the juice. São Paulo-based Cutrale (pictured) produces more than 20 per cent of global orange-juice supplies.

ABOVE Aerial view of the Agrishow in Ribeirão Preto, in São Paulo. This international agricultural technology fair, created in 1994, is considered the second largest fair of the industry in the world and the largest in Latin America.

ABOVE Employees at a meat processing plant owned by Brazil's JBS, the world's largest beef producer. Brazilians are great consumers of beef, eating up to 75 per cent of the country's annual production of more than 24.6 million tons. Brazil is also the world's number one exporter of beef.

ABOVE AND RIGHT In the 1980s, images showing the degrading conditions of workers in the gold mine of Serra Pelada gold mine, in Pará, shocked the world. More than 80,000 *garimpeiros* (prospectors) rushed to the area during the peak production period, but after numerous landslides and lack of enforcement of safety measures, the mine was closed. Recently, a Brazilian-Canadian joint venture was granted a licence to reopen Serra Pelada in mid-2013.

ABOVE Operators work in the port and railroad control room at the Ponta da Madeira Maritime Terminal, in the state of Maranhão, northern Brazil. The site was chosen as the terminus of the Carajás Railroad, where trains unload iron ore for shipping overseas. China, the US and Japan are among the main destinations.

ABOVE The mining sector accounts for a fifth of Brazil's total exports, with iron representing more than half of the country's production of minerals. Mining is still a major industry in Minas Gerais state, home of the eighteenth century gold rush, with iron ore mines such Serra Azul (pictured), managed by MMX.

RIGHT Geologists estimate that more than 100 different gemstones can be found in Brazil, and the state of Minas Gerais alone accounts for 25 per cent of the world's output of precious and semiprecious stones. Among the most easily found are diamonds, opals, aquamarines, emeralds, alexandrite, amethyst, topaz and tourmalines.

OVERLEAF A train operated by Vale, Brazil's biggest mineral exporter, crosses a bridge in Açailândia, in Maranhão. The Carajás Railroad transports iron ore from the world's largest mine and is the main lifeline of the country's iron industry.

LEFT An area of the Amazon rainforest that has been burnt clear in order to make room for cattle ranches.

PREVIOUS PAGE Although dams provide a clean alternative to fossil fuel sources, they are not without controversy. The latest construction underway is the Belo Monte Dam on the Xingu River in the eastern Amazon. Its creation would displace some 20,000 people, which has led to vocal protests both within Brazil (as pictured here) and in the international community.

LEFT A worker in plant where charcoal is produced from illegally harvested Amazon rainforest wood. According to a recent Greenpeace study, illegal wood charcoal is primarily used in Brazil to power smelters producing pig iron, which is used to make steel for industries in countries including the US.

TOP A truck transports illegally harvested Amazon rainforest logs on a road near the Araribóia Indigenous Reserve, in Maranhão. Illegal logging is among the chief threats to the Amazon. The rate of deforestation has declined in recent years; still more than one-fifth of the rainforest has been destroyed.

ABOVE Workers hold a ladder as they prepare to load charcoal produced from illegally harvested Amazon rainforest wood on a truck in Rondon do Pará.

RIGHT Real-time satellite monitoring and a better enforcement of environmental laws have helped Brazil to curb illegal deforestation in the Amazon in the past decade. During the 2009 UN Climate Change Conference in Copenhagen, Brazil has committed to reduce its carbon dioxide emissions by up to 38 per cent by 2020.

ABOVE The Brazilian attitude toward the Amazon has changed since union leader, rubber tapper and environmentalist Chico Mendes (1944–88) spoke out against illegal logging and the destruction of the rainforest. His assassination in his home in the state of Acre, at the hands of local ranchers, led to a public outcry that acted as a catalyst for a budding environmental movement.

RIGHT A former rubber tapper in Acre and a friend of Chico Mendes, Marina Silva scaled the political ranks from the local workers' union to a seat in the Senate. She was ex-President Luiz Inácio Lula da Silva's minister of environment for five years, but broke with him and his party, gathering almost 20 per cent of the votes in the 2010 presidential election. Since then, she has been internationally acclaimed as an ambassador for environmental issues.

Juntos pelo Bra

LEFT Originally built for the 1950 World Cup, when Brazil lost the trophy to Uruguay, the legendary Maracanã Stadium (pictured here in April 2013) has been completely renovated for the 2014 tournament. If the Brazilian squad makes it to the final match, it is here that it will play for its sixth world champion title.

ABOVE Scheduled to host the opening match of the 2014 World Cup, the Arena de São Paulo stadium (pictured here in 2011) will have a capacity for more than 65,000 spectators. Also known as *Itaquerão* for its location in the deprived Itaquera district of São Paulo, it will be used afterwards by the popular local club Corinthians.

ABOVE Brazilian fans watch the Bahia derby between Vitória and Esporte Clube Bahia at the official inauguration of the Arena Fonte Nova, Salvador, in April 2013. The original stadium of 1951 was demolished to make way for the new building, which has almost 49,000 seats.

TOP Overview of the work at Brasília's National Stadium, April 2013; the new stadium was built on the same site where the original Mané Garrincha arena stood. With 70,000 seats, it is only behind Maracanã in terms of capacity among the stadiums hosting the 2014 World Cup.

ABOVE Workers stand in the tunnel for the construction of Line 4 of the Rio de Janeiro underground system, February 2012. The line is to be completed ahead of the 2016 Olympic Games and is planned to reach the Barra da Tijuca neighbourhood in the west part of the city.

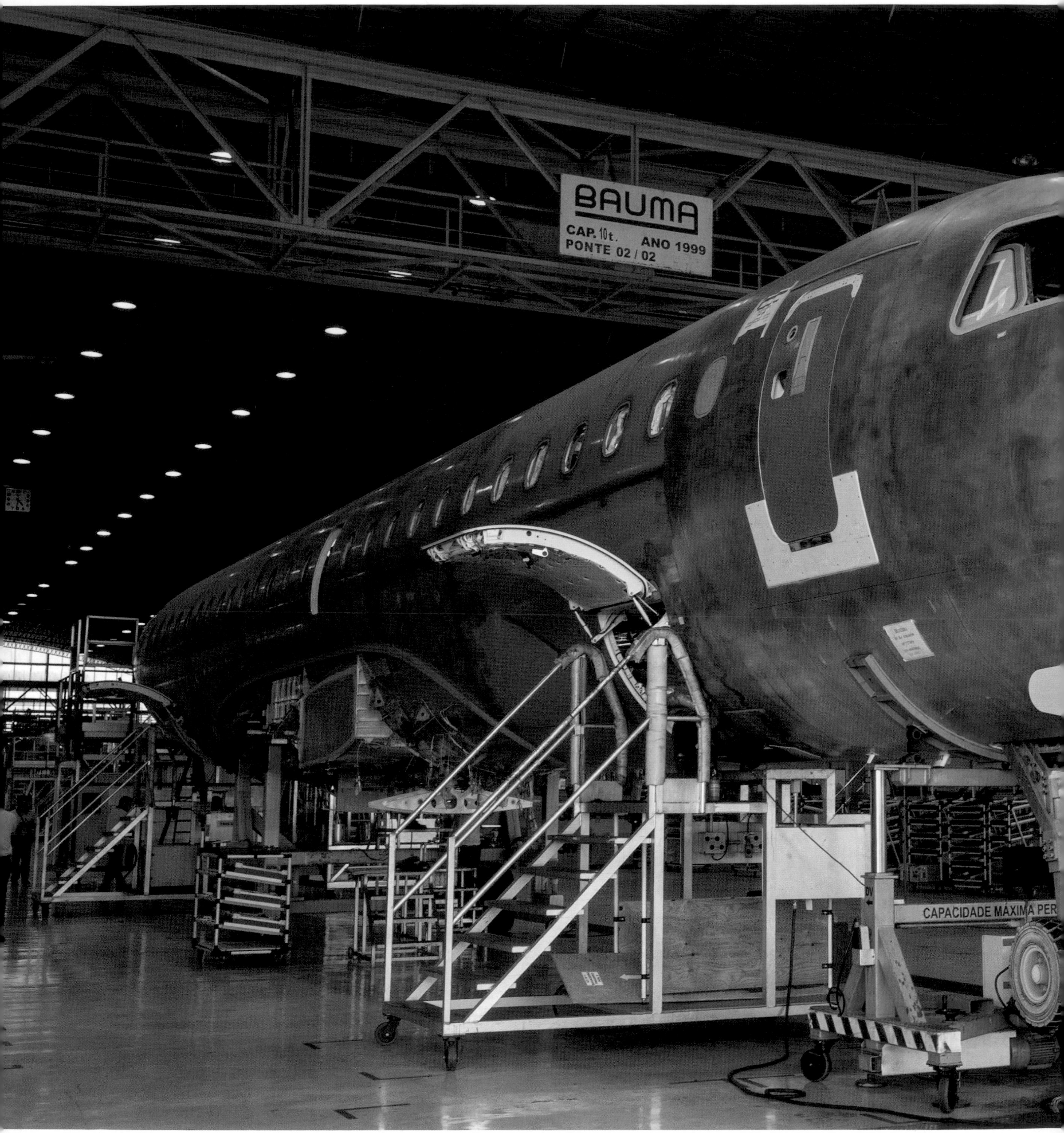
BAUMA
CAP. 10t. ANO 1999
PONTE 02 / 02
CAPACIDADE MÁXIMA PER

LEFT Based in São José dos Campos, about 100 km (62 miles) from São Paulo, aircraft maker Embraer is one of Brazil's most successful manufacturers. Founded as a state-run company in 1969, it was on the verge of bankruptcy when auctioned to private investors in 1994. Today, it is among the largest civil aircraft manufacturers in the world.

LEFT The Italian Isetta was licensed to a Brazilian machinery manufacturer in 1956 to become the country's first national car. Big multinationals, such as GM (pictured here in 2010), Volkswagen, Ford and Fiat installed their plants soon afterwards and never left the country. The Brazilian car industry is still growing, and today the country is among the world's largest producers.

ABOVE Wind farms, such as Beberibe, in the state of
Ceará (pictured), are still a rare sight in Brazil. Wind power
accounts for less than 1 per cent of the country's installed
electricity capacity, but a recent series of investments from
government and multinational companies may see up to a
seven-fold increase in the next few years, according to
independent analysts.

ABOVE Petroleo Brasileiro SA's P-51 oil platform stands in the Marlim Sul field, at the Campos Basin, approximately 90 miles (150 km) off the coast of the state of Rio de Janeiro. Created by the Vargas administration in 1953, state-controlled Petrobras is Brazil's largest company, with a market value in excess of US$290 billion.

TOP LEFT High-voltage power lines carry electricity from the Itaipu hydroelectric plant, which sits a short distance downstream from the Iguaçu Falls, in Paraná. Created in partnership with Paraguay, the dam provides almost 20 per cent of the electricity consumed in Brazil, and 90 per cent of that consumed in Paraguay.

BELOW LEFT One of the oldest commercial crops in Brazil, sugarcane has turned out to be a sustainable, energy-efficient fuel source. The country began developing its ethanol industry after the oil crisis of 1973, providing subsidies to sugar producers and encouraging manufacturers to make cars with engines that ran on the new fuel.

RIGHT A worker tests the quality of ethanol samples at Biosev's processing facility, near Sertãozinho, in the state of São Paulo. In 2003, new cars came out with "flex-fuel" engines, able to run on ethanol, petrol or any combination of the two. As a result, ethanol today accounts for about half of all fuel sales in Brazil.

BELOW RIGHT Brazil's mighty rivers hold vast potential in the realm of hydropower. More than 85 per cent of the electricity consumed in the country comes from hydropower sources. The massive Itaipu Dam (pictured), completed in 1984 at a cost of nearly US$20 billion, was the world's largest hydropower plant until the recent opening of China's Three Gorges Dam.

OVERLEAF Overview of the Angra 3 nuclear plant under construction in Angra dos Reis, Rio de Janeiro state, where two other pressurized water reactors have been operating since 1985. Nuclear energy generates only 3 per cent of Brazil's electricity and Angra is the country's sole plant, but the government has announced plans for the installation of new plants in the near future.

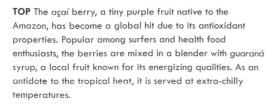

TOP The *açaí* berry, a tiny purple fruit native to the Amazon, has become a global hit due to its antioxidant properties. Popular among surfers and health food enthusiasts, the berries are mixed in a blender with *guaraná* syrup, a local fruit known for its energizing qualities. As an antidote to the tropical heat, it is served at extra-chilly temperatures.

ABOVE The influence of indigenous food is strong in the north of the country. Served in the rainforest region, *tacacá* is a cassava soup with sun-dried shrimp and *jambu* – a plant that has an anaesthetic effect on the mouth. Here, a Kayapó tribesman prepares to cook bushmeat in banana leaves.

ABOVE Whether in a *moqueca de peixe*, a fish stew from Bahia filled with African spices, or simply grilled and served as a snack along with a few beers and *caipirinhas* (the national cocktail), Brazil is renowned for its variety of fish and seafood, from the oceanic *bonito* to the sweet water *pirarucu*.

LEFT People shop for fish at the historic Ver-o-Peso market in Belém, Brazil. Belém is considered the entrance gate to the Amazon and for more than 300 years boats have unloaded their wares from deep in the Amazon at the market. Fishermen and others who make their livelihood on the waters of the Amazon basin face a variety of environmental hazards including pollution from mining, agricultural runoff and silting of the waters caused by deforestation. *Ver-o-peso* means "see the weight" and was named after the colonial Portuguese practice of weighing merchandise to be taxed for the Portuguese crown.

RIGHT Cattle owned by Brazilian beef producer Minerva SA graze in a ranch operated by Cia Agropecuária Monte Alegre (CMA) in Barretos.

TIMELINE

12,000 BC Human settlers travel across the Bering Land Bridge connecting Asia and North America and spread southward.

1494 Portugal and Spain sign the Treaty of Tordesillas, dividing future discoveries between them. eastern South America will fall to Portugal.

1500 Explorer Pedro Álvares Cabral makes landfall around present-day Porto Seguro and claims the land for the Portuguese crown.

1500s Introduced diseases from Europeans wipe out vast populations of indigenous tribes.

1534–36 The Portuguese king divides Brazil into 14 captaincies and hands them out to royal patrons. Only two become commercially successful.

1549 Brazil's first governor-general, Tomé de Sousa, is named. He centralizes authority and founds the city of Salvador, Brazil's colonial capital.

1550 Portugal begins raids on African villages and brings their human cargo to Brazil, where they are sold in open-air slave markets.

1621 The Dutch West India Company arrives in northeastern Brazil, in the hope of eventually taking control of the colony from Portugal.

1624 The Dutch invade and seize control of Salvador. They control the city for a year before being expelled by Portuguese troops.

1628 António Raposo Tavares, one of Brazil's most infamous *bandeirantes*, leads violent raids to capture and enslave Amerindians.

1637 Based in Recife, John Maurice of Nassau, Dutch prince and colonial governor, helps the Dutch gain control over northeastern Brazil.

1654 After a decade of war against the Dutch in Brazil, the Portuguese finally defeat Holland, ending their presence in Brazil.

1650s Communities of runaway slaves, known as *quilombos*, grow in the colony. Many will become official towns after abolition.

1690s Word spreads of the discovery of gold in present-day Minas Gerais, Mato Grosso, Goiás and southern Bahia.

1695 Palmares, the largest *quilombo* in Brazil, with over 20,000 inhabitants, is destroyed after decades of attacks by Portuguese troops.

1710 Huge boomtowns spring up in the gold regions, bringing tens of thousands of prospectors and slaves.

1727 The first coffee beans arrive in Brazil, allegedly introduced by a Brazilian army officer returning from French Guiana.

1740s Jesuit missionaries build São Miguel das Missões in southern Brazil to introduce Christianity to indigenous groups.

1750 In the Treaty of Madrid, Spain concedes vast territory to the Portuguese and demarcates Brazil's western borders, largely intact today.

1763 The Portuguese court transfers the capital of Brazil from Salvador to Rio de Janeiro.

1789 Brazilian revolutionary leader Tiradentes and a handful of conspirators attempt to bring independence. Their plot fails and Tiradentes is executed.

1805 Sculptor Antônio Francisco Lisboa (known as Aleijadinho) completes his masterpiece Os Profetas (The Prophets) in Congonhas, Minas Gerais.

1807 As Napoleon invades Portugal, the entire Portuguese court sails to Brazil and sets up in Rio.

1816 Dom João VI becomes king, declaring Rio the capital of the United Kingdom of Portugal and Brazil.

1816 Dom João VI invites the so-called French Mission of architects, artists and artisans to give Rio a European look.

1821 A financial crisis in Portugal prompts the King's departure. He leaves his son Pedro in charge of Brazil.

1822 Brazil's new overseer declares independence from Portugal, and proclaims himself emperor. So begins the rule of Dom Pedro I.

1830 Although slavery remains, slave trafficking is outlawed. Smuggling, however, brings 500,000 slaves to Brazil between 1830 and 1850.

1831 Dom Pedro I proves an incompetent ruler, and abdicates the throne, leaving power to his five-year-old son, Pedro II.

1831–40 With no central ruler and government in the hands of so-called *regências* (regencies), Brazil experiences widespread political turmoil.

1832 Charles Darwin spends several months in Rio during his epic South American voyage on the Beagle.

1835 Inspired by the earlier Haitian Revolution, Brazilian slaves in Salvador stage an uprising (the Malê Revolt), which narrowly fails.

1840 Aged just 15, Dom Pedro II becomes emperor, ushering in one of Brazil's most prosperous periods.

1850s The coffee bush flourishes in Brazil. *Fazendas* (ranches) spring up as Brazil becomes a major exporter of coffee.

1865 Allied with Uruguay and Argentina, Brazil wages war on Paraguay. This proves to be South America's bloodiest conflict, decimating the population of Paraguay.

1876 Englishman Henry Wickham smuggles 70,000 rubber-tree seeds out of Amazonia on a chartered freighter to London.

1888 Princess Isabel signs the law abolishing slavery. Brazil is the last country in the New World to ban it.

1888 More than 800,000 slaves, largely unskilled and illiterate, must fend for themselves: many come to urban areas.

1889 A military coup, supported by Brazil's wealthy coffee farmers, overthrows Pedro II. The monarchy is abolished.

1889: The Brazilian Republic is born. Little changes however, with power in the hands of the coffee oligarchs.

1890 Coffee powers Brazil's economy. The humble bean accounts for two-thirds of the country's exports.

1890 Demand for rubber explodes with the invention of the pneumatic tyre and the rise of the US automobile industry.

1890s Brazil opens its borders, welcoming a flood of immigrants from Italy, Spain and elsewhere.

1891 Pedro II, who left Brazil after being deposed, dies heartbroken in exile.

1893 Itinerant preacher Antônio Conselheiro and his followers found Canudos, a city that grows to a population of 35,000 in just two years.

1896 Funded by wealth from the rubber boom, the incredibly ornate Teatro Amazonas in Manaus opens.

1897 Fearful of plots against the government, federal troops invade and destroy Canudos.

1900 Brazil's cities are modernized, with the creation of grand boulevards and improvements in public health and sanitation.

1900 As the only natural exporter of rubber, Brazil booms, with fabled wealth brought to the Amazonian cities of Belém and Manaus.

1909 Modelled on the Palais Garnier in Paris, the lavish Teatro Municipal opens in Rio de Janeiro.

1910 Brazil's greatest explorer, Cândido Rondon, founds the Indian Protection Service. Its motto: "Die if necessary, but never kill".

1914 Cândido Rondon leads former US President Theodore Roosevelt on an exploration of a remote area of the Amazon basin.

1917 Samba is officially born, with the first recording of the song "Pelo Telefone".

1920 The rubber monopoly crashes, as the English and Dutch plant their own rubber trees in the East Indies.

1921 The remains of Pedro II are returned to Brazil in time for the centennial of Brazilian independence.

1922 Growing discontent with the political leadership. A military coup that erupts in Rio's Copacabana fails.

1922 Modern Art Week, held in São Paulo, heralds a groundbreaking new movement in the Brazilian art scene.

1923 The Copacabana Palace opens. The hotel becomes an icon of Rio's tropical glamour and of the roaring 1920s boom days.

1925 Famed British explorer Percy Fawcett disappears in Amazonia on his quest to discover an ancient lost city.

1927 Russo-Brazilian architect Gregori Warchavchik builds the first Modernist building in São Paulo, his own house.

1928 Deixa Falar becomes the first samba school (so-called because it is located next to a primary school).

1928 Poet Oswald de Andrade publishes Cannibal Manifesto, which describes the Brazilian appetite for other cultural movements from abroad.

1929 The stock market crash on Wall Street spells ruin for the coffee market as prices plummet.

1930 Shortly after Júlio Prestes becomes president, he is deposed, and Getúlio Vargas becomes Brazil's new "provisional" President.

1930 Classical composer Heitor Villa-Lobos creates Bachianas Brasileiras, a series of nine suites that pays homage to both the work of Johann Sebastian Bach and Brazilian folk music.

1931 The Cristo Redentor (Christ the Redeemer) statue is completed in Rio. It is considered the largest Art Deco monument in the world.

1932 Rio holds its first *carnaval* parade. Mangueira wins and soon becomes the city's favourite samba school.

1933 Sociologist Gilberto Freyre publishes *The Masters and the Slaves*, which provides an eye-opening account of Brazil's mixed-race heritage.

1936 Historian Sérgio Buarque de Holanda publishes *The Roots of Brazil*, a defining work in Brazilian scholarship.

1937 Inspired by European fascists, Getúlio Vargas announces a new constitution for what he calls the *Estado Novo* (New State).

1937 Vargas becomes Brazil's first president to wield absolute power. He bans political parties, imprisons opponents and censors the press.

1938 Vargas passes minimum wage laws and other labour initiatives that endear him to workers.

1938 Lampião, a bandit in the Northeast, is killed by police. He and his gang are later hailed as folk heroes.

1941 Austrian exile Stefan Zweig writes a bestseller about his newly adopted country entitled *Brazil: Country of the Future*.

1942 Despite Vargas' initial support for the fascists, Brazil joins the Allies in World War II, providing raw materials and 25,000 troops.

1950 Brazil hosts the World Cup. Rio's new Maracanã stadium attracts 200,000 fans to the final, which Brazil lost to Uruguay, 2 to 1.

1951 Despite his autocratic governance, Vargas remains popular and is reelected, this time democratically.

1953 President Getúlio Vargas creates the state-run oil company, Petrobras.

1954 The military calls for Vargas' resignation. He writes a final note before committing suicide by shooting himself in the heart.

1956 Architects Oscar Niemeyer and Lúcio Costa are tasked with designing a new capital from scratch.

1958 Brazil wins its first World Cup. The team wins largely due to the skills of a 17-year-old named Pelé.

1958 Bahian literary luminary Jorge Amado publishes *Gabriela, Clove and Cinnamon*, one of his finest works.

1960 President Juscelino Kubitschek moves the capital of Brazil from Rio to the newly-constructed city of Brasília.

1960s Artists create *tropicalismo*, a movement in music, visual arts and theatre that incorporates wide-ranging international influences.

1962 Brazilian musicians perform in New York City's Carnegie Hall, introducing bossa nova to a global audience.

1963 Glauber Rocha and other Brazilian filmmakers create *cinema novo*, expressive films addressing the country's major social problems.

1964 A military coup overthrows President João Goulart. So begins the era of dictatorship.

1964 A critic of the military dictatorship, architect Oscar Niemeyer flees the country and lives in Paris until 1985.

1964 Singer-composer Chico Buarque makes his public debut. Later he becomes one of Brazil's best-loved songwriters.

1965 Roberto Marinho founds his Globo media empire. By 2012, it is the second-largest commercial TV network in the world.

1967 The National Security Law is passed, which leads to the jailing, torture and murder of political dissidents.

1968 Led by Caetano Veloso and Gilberto Gil, *Tropicália* is born in July — a movement criticizing the military dictatorship.

1968 Institutional Act 5 is passed in December. It purges opposition parties from public office and bans most political parties.

1968 In response to repressive laws, in December protests erupt nationwide. Over 100,000 take to the streets of Rio.

1968 Despite the military dictatorship, the Brazilian economy booms, averaging 10 per cent annual growth over the next six years.

1968–72 After several months in jail, Veloso and Gil go into exile in London, where they continue performing.

1970 Marxist group member Dilma Rousseff is arrested and held in prison for almost three years, where she is allegedly tortured.

1972 In an era of runaway deficits, Brazil spends US$1 billion on the 5,300-km (3,293-mile) Trans-Amazonian highway, never completed.

1973 Following the worldwide oil crisis, Brazil invests heavily in biofuels. Sugarcane proves to be a remarkable energy source.

1979–80 Continuing decline of workers' wages leads to nationwide strikes. Unions lead the call for political reform.

1980 A union leader named Lula helps found the Partido dos Trabalhadores (Workers' Party), attracting workers, academics and environmentalists.

1980 Lula's criticism of the military regime and his involvement in organizing strikes lands him in prison for a month.

1981 The release of Pixote, a film that depicts the tragic lives of street youth in Brazil.

1984 Movimento Sem Terra (MST – Landless Workers' Movement), an organization calling for land reform, is founded.

1984 Itaipu becomes the world's largest hydropower plant. It provides 20 per cent of Brazil's electricity and 90 per cent of Paraguay's.

1985 Brazil holds an indirect presidential election. When Tancredo Neves wins, millions of Brazilians celebrate the end of dictatorship.

1985 Neves dies of complications following abdominal surgery before taking office. His vice-presidential candidate, José Sarney, is sworn in as president.

1988 Paulo Coelho publishes The Alchemist, one of the world's most successful novels; it will go on to sell over 30 million copies.

1988 Amazonia rubber tappers' leader and environmentalist Chico Mendes is murdered by local ranchers.

1989 Public outcry and shock following Mendes' death compels the Brazilian government to create extractive reserves.

1989 After four years in office, President José Sarney proves incapable of taming the spiralling inflation inherited from his predecessors.

1989 Brazil holds its first direct presidential election. Fernando Collor de Mello, governor from a small northeastern state, wins.

1990 Brazil's economy remains in dire straits. The external debt stands at a crippling US$115 billion.

1994 President Collor de Mello is accused of corruption on a vast scale. Following a congressional inquiry, he is eventually impeached.

1994 Found not guilty of "passive corruption" by the Supreme Court, Collor de Mello moves to Miami.

1994 After Collor de Mello's impeachment, Vice President Itamar Franco assumes the presidency.

1994 Three-time Formula One champion Ayrton Senna da Silva is killed in the San Marino Grand Prix.

1994 Rio's Favela-Bairro project is created, earmarking US$180 million (£116 million) for poor communities over the next decade.

1994 Franco introduces a new currency, the real, which stabilizes the economy and ushers in an economic boom.

1994 Inflation plummets from a rate of over 5,000 per cent in late 1993 to below 10 per cent in 1994.

1998 After five years in the US, Collor de Mello returns to Brazil and attempts to reenter politics.

2002 Following three unsuccessful attempts, former union leader Luíz Inácio "Lula" da Silva succeeds in winning the presidency.

2002 Brazil wins its fifth World Cup title, beating Germany 2 to 0 in the final.

2002 The acclaimed film City of God is released. Brazil's dire social problems reach a global audience.

2003 President Lula launches the Bolsa Família program of cash transfers to 11 million of Brazil's poorest families.

2003 Musician Gilberto Gil is named Brazil's minister of culture, a post in which he will serve until 2008.

2003 Volkswagen do Brasil releases the Gol 1.6 Total Flex car, with an engine capable of running on ethanol, petrol or any combination of the two.

2005 Brazil repays its entire US$15 billion (£9.7 billion) debt to the International Monetary Fund (IMF) ahead of schedule.

2005 Dorothy Stang, an American missionary nun and vocal supporter of rainforest inhabitants, is murdered by a local rancher.

2006 Following several unsuccessful political comebacks, disgraced former president Collor de Mello is elected as a senator for Alagoas.

2006 Despite a widespread bribery scandal in his party, Lula is reelected as president.

2006 Brazil becomes energy-independent, achieving self-sufficiency in crude oil.

2006 Brazilian architect Paulo Mendes da Rocha receives the Pritzker Prize for his innovative work.

2007 Rio successfully hosts the Pan American Games, spending an estimated US$2 billion (£1.3 billion).

2007 Brazil wins the right to host the 2014 FIFA World Cup.

2007 A Brazilian expedition pinpoints a new source of the Amazon, some 6,800 km (4,225 miles) from the Atlantic Ocean.

2009 Rio outbids Chicago and other cities to host the 2016 Summer Olympics.

2009 Researchers discover the earliest-known rock art in the Americas (over 10,000 years old) in Central Brazil.

2010 Rio unveils Porto Maravilha (Marvellous Port), a massive R$8 billion (£5.2 billion) project to transform a derelict waterfront.

2010 Bilateral trade soars under Lula's watch to US$25 billion (£16.4) by the end of his presidency.

2010 After two terms as President, Lula leaves office with record-high approval ratings.

2010 Brazil's annual growth rate is 7.5 per cent, the nation's highest level in 25 years.

2010 According to the national census, around 6 per cent of Brazilians (over 11 million people) live in *favelas*.

2010 Dilma Rousseff is elected president, becoming the first female head of state in Brazil's history.

2012 Rio's *carnaval* continues to break records, with over 1 million visitors, and revenues of over US$700 million (£451 million).

2012 At the grand age of 104, Oscar Niemeyer dies. He is hailed as one of the great architects of the twentieth century.

2013 According to the International IMF, Brazil is the world's seventh-largest economy.

2013 Despite protests, Brazil greenlights the Belo Monte dam, which will flood Amazonian rainforest and displace 20,000 people.

2014 Brazil hosts the World Cup, spending an incredible US$13.7 billion (£8.8 billion) in preparation for the event.

2016 Rio hosts the Summer Olympics, becoming the first South American country in history to stage the event.

INDEX

CREDITS

The publishers would like to thank Getty Images for their kind permission to reproduce the pictures in this book.

272, 273; /Robert Nickelsberg/Time & Life Pictures: 56, 57; /Gaspar Nobrega/Inovafoto/
LatinContent: 270; /Adenilson Nunes/LatinContent: 192-193; /Cesar Okada: 190-191; /
Herbert Orth/Time Life Pictures: 48; /Per-Gunnar Ostby: 203 (bottom); /Lunae Parracho/
LatinContent: 82-83; /Mino Pedrosa/Globo: 59 (top); /Hipolito Pereira/Globo: 55 (bottom); /
John Phillips/Time Life Pictures: 46 (bottom), 86, 90 (bottom), 91 (left); /Ryan Pierse: 159
(left), 160; /Christopher Pillitz: 147; /Spencer Platt: 246; /Viviane Ponti: 275 (bottom); /Paul
Popper/Popperfoto: 49 (top); /Popperfoto: 151 (bottom), 152; /Pictorial Parade: 53 (top); /
Julio Pereira/AFP: 60; /Mondadori Portfolio: 85; /Rich Press/Bloomberg: 275 (top), 297; /
Hart Preston: 143; /Hart Preston/Time & Life Pictures: 226-227; /Prisma/UIG: 21, 38; /Nilton
Sergio Ramos Quoirin: 178-179; /Michael Regan: 224-225; /Ricardo Ribas/Latin Content: 87
(top); /Alex Robinson: 191, 198-199; /Roger Viollet Collection: 26, 43, 68, 88-89; /Jean-
Regis Rouston/Roger Viollet: 238; /Sean Rowland/ASP: 159 (right); /Ted Russell/Time Life
Pictures: 52; /SSPL: 34-35; /Evaristo SA/AFP: 73 (centre), 291 (top); /Alex Saberi: 199 (top);
/Jewel Samad/AFP: 62; /SambaPhoto/Pablo Di Giulio: 13, 120, 121 (top); /SambaPhoto/
Angelo Maciel: 240 (bottom); /Luiz Carlos Frota Sampaio: 174-175; /Rainer W. Schlegelmilch:
156 (top); /Peter Schoen: 201 (bottom), 203 (top); /Antonio Scorza/AFP: 12, 58-59, 64, 65
(top), 73 (top), 74-75, 104, 124, 142 (bottom), 170-171, 182 (bottom), 286; /David
Silverman: 298 (top); /Christophe Simon/AFP: 77 (bottom), 116-117, 122, 128-129, 132, 141
(bottom), 217 (top), 248-249; /Mauricio Simonetti: 214, 234-235; /Gerard Sioen/Gamma-
Rapho: 212-213, 238-239; /Jan Sochor/Latincontent: 80-81, 125, 127 (top), 129 (top); /
Otavio de Souza/LatinContent: 10, 118-119; /Renata Souza e Souza: 185, 202 (bottom); /
Boris Streubel/Bongarts: 158; /Babek Tafreshi/SSPL: 197 (top); /Mario Tama: 72, 95 (bottom),
97, 110, 119 (top), 154-155, 252, 276-277, 278-279, 282, 283 (top), 283 (bottom), 304-

305; /Tambako the Jaguar: 199 (bottom); /Robin Tenison: 260-261; /Bob Thomas: 150; /Three
Lions: 242; /Time Life Pictures/Mansell/Time Life Pictures: 36; /Topical Press Agency/Hulton
Archive: 228; /Universal History Archive: 25 (top); /Universal Images Group: 264, 280-281; /
Jose Varella/AFP: 59 (bottom); /Luis Veiga: 267 (top); /Thiago Veras: 250-251; /Ari Versiani/
AFP: 100-101, 130-131; /William Volcov/News Free/LatinContent: 155 (centre); /Luciana
Whitaker/LatinContent: 181 (bottom); / Doelan Yann: 221; /Dario Zalis/Contexto: 126 (top)

Every effort has been made to acknowledge correctly and contact the source and/or copyright
holder of each picture and Carlton Books Limited apologises for any unintentional errors or
omissions, which will be corrected in future editions of this book.

BIBLIOGRAPHY

Bellos, Alex. *Futebol: Soccer, The Brazilian Way*. New York: Bloomsbury USA, 2002.

Fausto, Boris. *A Concise History of Brazil*. Cambridge: Cambridge University Press, 1999.

Hemming, John *Tree of Rivers: The Story of the Amazon*. London: Thames and Hudson, 2008.

Kricher, John C. *A Neotropical Companion: An Introduction to the Animals, Plants and Ecosystems of the New World Tropics*. Princeton: Princeton University Press, 1997.

Levine, Robert M. *The History of Brazil*. Westport, Connecticut: Greenwood Press, 1999.

Page, Joseph A. *The Brazilians*. Reading, Massachusetts: Perseus Books, 1995.

Rohter, Larry. *Brazil on the Rise: The Story of a Country Transformed*. New York: Palgrave Macmillan, 2010.

Skidmore, Thomas E. *Brazil: Five Centuries of Change*. New York: Oxford University Press, 1999.

—— *Politics in Brazil 1930–1964: An Experiment in Democracy*. New York: Oxford University Press, 1967.

Vincent, Jon S. *Culture and Customs of Brazil*. Westport, Connecticut: Greenwood Press, 2003.